COLORADO
MOUNTAIN CLUB
PACK GUIDE

THE BEST
URBAN
HIKES:
DENVER

CHRIS ENGLERT

The Colorado Mountain Club Press

Golden, Colorado

The Best Urban Hikes: Denver
© 2017 by The Colorado Mountain Club

PUBLISHED BY

The Colorado Mountain Club Press
710 10th Street, Suite 200, Golden, CO 80401
303-996-2743   email: cmcpress@cmc.org
website: http://www.cmc.org

Founded in 1912, The Colorado Mountain Club is the largest outdoor recreation, education, and conservation organization in the Rocky Mountains. Look for our books at your local bookstore or outdoor retailer or online at www.cmc.org/books.

Rebecca Finkel: book designer
Mira Perrizo: copy editor
Clyde Soles: publisher

CORRECTIONS: We greatly appreciate when readers alert us to errors or outdated information by emailing cmcpress.org

DISTRIBUTED TO THE BOOK TRADE BY:
Mountaineers Books, 1001 SW Klickitat Way, Suite 201, Seattle, WA 98134, 800-553-4453, www.mountaineersbooks.org

TOPOGRAPHIC MAPS courtesy of CalTopo.com.

COVER PHOTO: Thornton holds many treasures for great urban hikes, and it's nearby too.

We gratefully acknowledge the financial support of the people of Colorado through the Scientific and Cultural Facilities District of greater metropolitan Denver for our publishing activities.

Printed in Korea
ISBN 978-1-937052-52-2

OVERVIEW MAP

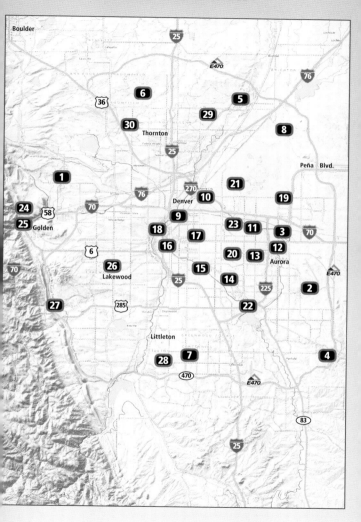

CONTENTS

The Platte River.

THE BEST URBAN HIKES: DENVER

Preface

I couldn't sleep. It was May of 2014, and my family and I had just returned from a 30-day, around-the-world adventure. Passing through 24 time zones in 30 days had messed up my sleep cycle, so at 2:00 a.m., I put on my walking shoes and ventured out into my Denver neighborhood. In the crisp spring air, my thoughts ran to all the walking and urban hiking we had just done. Every day, the three of us had laced up our most comfortable shoes and explored the world, one step at a time. We connected—with ourselves, with each other, and with literally the world around us. The feeling of connection wouldn't escape me. How could I keep it going?

I vowed to keep walking. Regardless of the pressure of work, raising a family, and the demands of life, I'd carve out a daily walk. And this vow, this commitment to daily walking, quickly unleashed a passion that was just waiting to emerge. I had always been a walker—I credit my parents for requiring me to walk the half-mile every day to the bus stop and back—but I had never really owned my love for it. It was time to step it up and step out into the world.

For the next year I walked every block of my neighborhood. I joined Walk2Connect, a Denver-based walking co-op, and began leading walks. I discovered that other folks liked walking too. Together we found new neighborhoods, embraced the trails of Denver, and ventured into alleys, parks, and streets. Walking, not driving, opened doors of enjoyment and connection. Soon I couldn't imagine not walking and exploring every day.

My blog, *UrbanHikingDen.com*, exploded with reader questions asking where to walk. When I wrote about my adventures, people wrote back. Who were these folks? They were people, just like you and me, who wanted to walk. My readers wanted advice on where to go, how to access trails, and what shoes to wear. Bored with their own neighborhood walks, they wanted to get out and explore Denver. The central reader question was, "Where should we start?"

The High Line Canal Trail.

THE BEST URBAN HIKES: DENVER

So I wrote this book. For all of you in Denver who don't want to spend time on I-70 to get to mountain hiking, who don't have the time to spend driving to some adrenaline-pumping, elevation-changing climb, who want to quickly jump on a trail and explore Denver, this book is for you. It's urban hiking in our beloved Denver.

Imagine drawing a circle around Denver that roughly follows C-470/E-470. All 30 hikes in this book fall within that circle. These are the best hikes in Denver—meaning you can find one of the many trailheads within 10 minutes from your Denver home and away from traffic. No need to buy hiking gear, special boots, or hydration packs. These hikes are accessible, convenient, and family friendly. Some will challenge you due to elevation gain or length, but all invite the urban hiker to come out and explore the best of Denver—by foot.

It's time to connect. See you on the trail,

Chris

Aurora's Norfolk Glen. Thank you to Robbin Mitchell for sharing this hike.

To my granddaddy who walked with my mom, and to my mom who walked with me, "mock orange."

THE BEST URBAN HIKES: DENVER

Introduction

When people think about hiking in Denver, they naturally jump their thoughts to the Rocky Mountains and the grand hiking that happens in our beautiful mountains. But why? Right here in Denver, within the C-470 loop, are hundreds of miles of trails and hundreds of parks. Most homes in metro Denver sit just minutes from a park or trail. So instead of jumping in a car and braving I-70 to the mountains, why not take advantage of the richness of Denver's trail and park system?

A VARIETY OF URBAN HIKES

First, exactly what is an urban hike? How does it differ from a walk in the city or a hike in the woods? An urban hike is a trek within an urban environment that probably includes a defined trail and/or a park, and it may be on hard or soft surfaces. So why write a book about urban hikes within Denver?

In Denver alone, there are over a hundred parks. Add in the outlying suburbs of Littleton, Aurora, Golden, Thornton, Arvada, and Wheat Ridge, that number doubles. Connecting many of these parks is the regional trail system of at least 20 major trails and many smaller tributaries off of them. The 71-mile High Line Canal Trail, arguably the first "official" trail in the system, takes walkers from Waterton Canyon to Green Valley Ranch. The Mary Carter Trail, arguably the shortest at 10 miles, takes hikers along the southern portion of the Platte River. But regardless of age or length, somehow the trails all connect, providing Denver urban hikers with plenty of ambling right here in the city.

The 30 hikes in this book give choices. From short 2.5-mile treks to a long 41-mile urban loop, these urban hikes invite all ages and abilities outside. The major trails are covered, and a few hidden trails are included. From Thornton to Littleton, Golden to Aurora, you'll get a good feel for the variety of Denver metro's landscapes, waterways, and escapades. Every walk in this book quickly takes you from the feel of the city and its noise to quiet, adventure, and discovery within a few miles of any neighborhood in Denver.

USING THIS BOOK

At the beginning of each hike, you'll find information about the elevation gain, difficulty, distance and time. Most of the walks in this book are flat. A few have some elevation gain, and those gains are usually geared to one spot on the trail that goes up a hill. Yet even though there is minimal elevation gain, the elevation is always at least 5280 feet. Thus, if you're not used to Denver's height, but sure to take care, listen to your body, and drink lots of water.

As for the rating, if the walk gets longer than 5 miles, the rating moves from easy to moderate. If there is elevation gain, the route moves to difficult. Finally, the distance comes from actually walking the route and using Google to measure on maps. The time is based on walking a mile in 20 minutes. Breaks are not factored into overall time.

SOME CAUTIONS

With urban hiking in Denver, you won't have to worry about wild animals or needing a rescue team to find you lost in the woods. But there are a few unique items and concerns to think about when urban hiking in Denver.

1. **Bring more water than you think you'll need.** The high elevation will make you thirstier quicker, and often while on the trails there are no public facilities to find fresh water. In addition, many of the restrooms and water faucets in the parks and on the trails are shut off in the winter.

2. **Invest in a good, small backpack or as a waist pack.** Carry your water and a snack with you, freeing up your hands for taking pictures.

3. **Make sure you wear good walking shoes.** Some man-ufacturers offer urban hiking shoes that are made for concrete and dirt surfaces, both of which you'll find plenty of while following these routes.

4. **Be sure your clothing is comfortable and breathable.** If you're not already wearing outerwear, be sure to throw a windbreaker into your day pack. Bring along a good hat and sunscreen, too.

5. **Have a good transit app on your phone.** Google does a great job providing public transit details. You might also want to download the Denver GO app and the RTD Transit Watch app. In addition, consider using Lyft or Uber for your one-way hikes where you need a ride back to your starting point.

6. **If you're walking alone, be sure to tell a friend** where you're walking and your estimated time to return.

7. **Consider bringing a personal defense system** such as: pepper spray, one-handed knife, flashlight, tactical pen, or whistle. Although all of the routes in this book are safe, having a way to defend one's self is a good idea.

8. **Carry a first-aid kit** with you, especially on the longer routes. You'll want to have blister prep materials and sunscreen.

9. **Seek out the park rangers on the trails.** You'll find them often on bikes. Engage in conversation and uncover any local information about the trails that might help you on the day you're hiking.

10. **Check the WalkRide Colorado website** (http://www.walkridecolorado.com/by-location/regional-trail-map) for updated information and new trails. Also join the Facebook page, Colorado Front Range Trail Conditions, for current views on local trails. Follow the rangers on Twitter for live updates from the trails.

11. **Wear a sportcam.** Not only will you get fun footage of your hike, but a small video camera can help deter folks from approaching you and can provide evidence if necessary.

12. **Most of the hikes in this book go on the regional trail system,** which cyclist use as well. So be sure you're never walking more than two abreast and if you have a dog, keep the dog on a 6-foot leash or less. When a cyclist approaches from behind, veer to the right as you hear "on your left," and don't wear headphones.

13. **Be aware of coyotes and snakes,** especially if you're walking with a dog. For coyotes, be big. Make noise, throw rocks, scare the coyote away. With snakes, keep your distance. If you're walking through prairie dog fields with your dog (all trails in this book require leashed dogs), keep your dog on the trail away from the holes. The prairie dog fleas can carry bubonic plague.

Some maps you might want to carry with you include the following:

Bicycling the Greater Denver Area Route Map by Denver Bicycle Touring Club

City of Westminster Trail Guide by Westminster Open Space

Denver Bike Map by City and County of Denver

Denver Parks by City and County of Denver

The Northeast Neighborhood Map by Northeast Connections

Park, Trail & Open Space by City of Aurora

Park, Trail & Open Space System Map & Guide by Commerce City

Regardless of which urban hike you pick, or if you pick them all, enjoy yourself. Post pictures, tag them with #urbanhikingDEN, and send us comments about the routes. We'd love to hear from you.

No need to venture to the Rockies for a good hike, there are plenty right here in Denver.

1. Arvada: Ralston Creek

RATING	Easy
DISTANCE	4.3 miles
TIME	1.5 hours
ELEVATION GAIN	Minimal
USAGE	Part of the regional trail system, you'll find walkers, bikers and joggers along this route.

COMMENTS: The Ralston Creek Trail is a beauty, traveling a healthy length of Arvada and includes Tucker Lake and Blunn Reservoir. Its eastern end adds the fun, suspended Gold Strike Bridge on its way into downtown Arvada, where gold was first discovered in Colorado. For this route, you start in the middle and work your way west through giant cottonwoods as you amble along the wiggly Ralston Creek. Arriving at the western end of this route, you can get super glimpses of Golden's North Table Mountain and then, if you'd like, you can decide to continue to the north up the side of the reservoir and around Tucker Lake, adding another 1.5 miles. If you're really ambitious, you can throw in the loop around the reservoir, adding another 2–3 miles. Regardless of how far you go, the route identified here offers good shade, great chances to see wildlife, and fun, old cottonwood snags that have fallen, providing interesting looks into their root systems.

GETTING THERE: Take Ward Road—CO 72 north to 64th Avenue —CO 72, turn left/west and continue to Indiana Street— CO 72, turn right/north and continue on 68th Avenue. Turn left/west, take the next right, Joyce Street, and follow around to 6833 before the bridge over the trail.

THE ROUTE: Park along Joyce Street and approach the trail from the west side of the street. You'll immediately find yourself on the trail next to the babbling Ralston Creek. The trail wiggles along, passing through designated wildlife areas. You'll walk over a small pedestrian bridge and see signs for the Croke Canal. On your right, you'll see an overflow structure of cement spikes, allowing the canal to spill into Ralston Creek. The Croke Canal, built in the late 1880s, moves water from Clear Creek to Standley Lake to service the water needs of Westminster, Thornton, Northglenn, and Arvada.

Cross over the canal and continue meandering along the trail. You'll get your first glimpse of West Woods Golf Course as you make your way across a bridge for golf carts. Cross the water and enter into a wildlife habitat area, and quickly you'll cross another bridge, passing tees #14 and #17. Once again, you'll cross over Croke Canal. This time look to your left for the wheels to the head gates that control the water flow through the canal.

> **The Croke Canal**
> An important part of Denver's water system, the Croke Canal draws water from Clear Creek between Golden's North and South Table Mountains. It then mixes with the Farmer's High Line Canal on the way to Standley Lake. The Farmers Reservoir and Irrigation Company (FRICO) owns the Croke Canal, and the cities of Westminster, Northglenn and Thornton jointly fund it. The Canal is named after Thomas Croke, a one-time Daniels & Fisher clerk who invested his savings well in land development in the 1880s. His land and orchards needed water, which ultimately led to him developing the canal and Standley Lake. As a Colorado State Senator, he also built a large mansion at Pennsylvania and E 11th Avenue in Capitol Hill, now rumored to be one of the most haunted homes in the area.

You'll come out of the woods and parallel West Woods Circle for just a few hundred feet along the sidewalk, and then you'll duck back along the golf course, going under Quaker Street. Rising out of the tunnel, notice the sign telling you to take a U-turn. You'll make a sharp left and walk back on top of Quaker Street, heading north, to catch Ralston Creek Trail up on the left. Watch for signs.

The Croke Canal.

Now that you're back on the trail on the north side of the creek, continue west. For a brief time you'll be in between two tees, but follow the Ralston Creek signs and you'll soon find yourself back along the creek and back into wildlife habitat. Cross the golf cart path, and up on your left you'll see bathrooms, which are open during the summer months. Walk to the right of the bathrooms, where the fairway will be on your right. Continue through the underpass at Virgil Way.

As you come out of the underpass, here is where you have choices. If you go right, you'll go up the steep climb of the backside of Blumm Reservoir. On that portion of the Ralston Creek Trail, you can decide to make a 1.5-mile loop around Tucker Lake and/or make a larger loop around the reservoir. Or, you can look left and get a nice view of North Table Mountain.

For this route, look left. Follow the trail to the left, crossing Virgil Way and veering to the right to make a loop back to the trail before it goes through the underpass you just walked through. You'll be back on Ralston Creek Trail, except this time you'll be facing east. From here, continue back the way you came, remembering to veer to the left at the restrooms on your way back to where you parked.

Indiana Street

72

TRAILHEAD

MILES

1.0

0 .1 .2 .3 .4 .5

2. Aurora: Eastern Aurora Buckley

RATING	Moderate
DISTANCE	7.0 miles
TIME	2.5 hours
ELEVATION	285 feet
USAGE	Meandering through the neighborhoods, you'll find walkers, bikers and joggers along this route. Along the Conservation Center Trail, you might find mountain bikers.

COMMENTS: The eastern edge of Aurora abuts the high plains. Out on this very eastern edge of the Denver metro area, just on the inside of the E-470 loop, is the area where no one ever thought growth would reach. Buckley Air Force Base dominates the landscape, the Denver landfill creates a high point, and the Plains Conservation Center fights to hold onto the last remaining prairie homesteads of the area. Nonetheless, with rolling hills, good sidewalks, and a soft trail that parallels the Plains Conservation Center, aviation lovers can enjoy both the Air Force jets and the birdlife of the plains in this 7-mile meander through eastern Aurora.

GETTING THERE: Start at Great Plains Park, which is at the intersection of E. Jewell Avenue and S. Genoa Street in Aurora, 20100 E Jewell Ave, Aurora. Take I-225 to Iliff Avenue. Turn east and go 4 miles. The park at 20100 E Jewell Ave, Aurora, will be on the south side of the road. Park in the parking lot, which has a compost toilet, spray park, and tot lot.

Aurora abuts the plains at the Conservation Plains Center.

THE ROUTE: This loop route can be traveled in either direction. If you want to get the noisier part of the loop out of the way and enjoy the Plains Conservation Center near the end of the hike, follow these directions. Otherwise, go in reverse, stopping at the Center earlier in your walk.

You'll begin the walk by walking along the south side of Jewell Avenue for about 0.3 mile along a well-paved sidewalk past homes. You'll walk up a gentle hill, then down to the intersection of Jewell and S. Dunkirk Street. Turn left and walk for about a mile up and down gentle hills, past a school on your right. Houses will frame both sides of the street, and the sidewalk meanders nicely along shaded areas. Dunkirk turns into Sterling Hills Parkway, which you'll continue on downhill until you reach Tower Road. Turn left along the sidewalk and walk a short distance to cross over Unnamed Creek Trail. Turn left.

You'll now be on the Unnamed Creek Trail, with the creek on your left and homes on your right. With cattails, cottonwoods, willows, and tall grasses growing along the creek, enjoy a 1.5-mile meander along the creek. When crossing Bates, look for the trail to jump to the north side, and at the Flanders crossing, follow the trail's jump to the south side of the creek. At E. Hampden Avenue, you'll walk through the tunnel then loop up to E. Hampden Avenue. Head east along Hampden to the first intersection at Himalaya Street. Cross the street so that you're on the north side and continue 0.75 mile east on Hampden to S. Conservatory Parkway.

At this point, you can either cross S. Conservatory Parkway and go to the Plains Conservation Center or cross S. Conservatory Parkway and take an immediate left so you're walking north on the east side of S. Conservatory Parkway. If you choose to enjoy the Center, you'll be treated to sod homes, teepees, and a general view into what life was like on the prairie in the late 1800s. Once you've had your fill at the Center, return back to S. Conservatory Parkway to the west. The trails within the Center only exit out of the grounds at the entrance. There are no access points from the street to the trails, so you must leave the Center to continue this walk.

Head north on S Conservatory Parkway. In about 200 yards, the sidewalk will fork. Take the right fork and you'll transition to a soft surface trail that parallels the Conservation Plains. From this vantage point, and for the next 2 miles, you'll be able to spy hawks, eagles, kestrels, flickers, pronghorn antelope, prairie dogs, and maybe a coyote or a fox. You may also see Buckley Air Force Base pilots practicing maneuvers in jets and helicopters. The soft surface will end just south of the approach to Great Plains Park. You'll be back on a sidewalk again, which you'll follow around to the right past the ball field. Take a left on the pebble trail and return back to the parking lot.

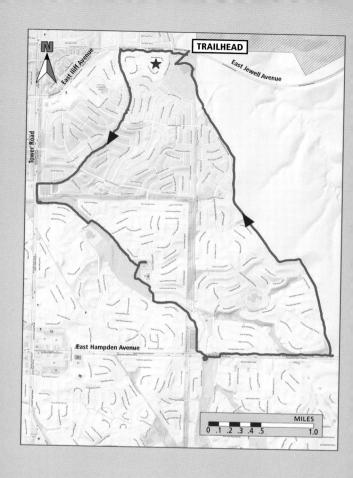

TRAILHEAD

East Jewell Avenue

East Iliff Avenue

Tower Road

N

East Hampden Avenue

MILES
0 .1 .2 .3 .4 .5   1.0

3. Aurora: Norfolk Glen Loop

RATING	Easy
DISTANCE	5 miles
TIME	2 hours
ELEVATION GAIN	Minimal
USAGE	Part of the regional trail system, you'll find walkers, bikers and joggers along this route.

COMMENTS: Although this route crosses over Colfax twice, you'd never know you were so close to Denver's major urban east-west corridor. Nestled in with Star K Ranch is the Norfolk Glen, a nature area and open space playing home to deer, fox, coyote, prairie dog, and a host of birds of prey. This is a geographically interesting hike, as it connects the Sand Creek Trail that runs southeast to northwest through Aurora and Stapleton with the High Line Canal, which runs from Green Valley Ranch to Waterton Canyon. Although there are restrooms at the trailhead and a portable toilet halfway through the route, there are no facilities even though you're only 0.5 mile from restaurants and shops throughout the entire walk—but you'd never know it.

GETTING THERE: Take I-70 to Airport Road and turn south on Airport. Go west (right) on Smith Road, then take a left on Laredo Street. Veer to the right at Star K Ranch. Park in the lot at the Morrison Nature Center, 16002 E. Smith Road, Aurora.

THE ROUTE: Park at the nature center then find any of the trailheads toward the Sand Creek Trail. Preferably, you'll choose the trailhead closest to the nature center. Walk south on the dirt trail and take a left on Sand Creek—you'll know it by the signs and how the trail becomes wide and pebbly. Go left and in about 100 yards, watch for a sign that says High Line Canal Connector. Turn right on the connector and walk about 0.5 mile through the glen, crossing over the Sand Creek via a small footbridge. Watch for several deer families in the high brush.

The connector ends at the High Line Canal Trail. Go left. The trail continues to the east with the Norfolk Glen on your left and its neighborhood on the right. In between the two, you'll see the High Line Canal paralleling you as you walk the trail. Although it no longer moves water from the Platte through here, you may see some water from rain collection or storm water runoff.

You'll reach Airport Road. Here, you can either cross Airport over the poorly marked crossing area, or go south half a block and use the crosswalks at the intersection of Airport/Colfax to cross.

If you cross over Airport, you'll cut diagonally to Colfax, and then you'll cross Colfax on a poorly marked crossing. Or, if you choose to cross Airport at the intersection, you'll also cross Colfax. Either way, once you've crossed over Airport and Colfax, you'll continue moving southeasterly along the High Line Canal Trail. Notice the ranch and stables just to the south of the trail. At this point, the canal will be on your left and the stables on your right.

You'll come to the Triple Creek Trailhead. Take a left, cross over Sand Creek and take another left. You'll now be on the Sand Creek Trail, walking northwesterly. There may be a portable

The High Line Canal Trail, Denver's oldest regional trail, follows the High Line Canal for 71 miles from Waterton Canyon in the south to its northern terminus in Green Valley Ranch. You can walk the entire trail, passing through rural areas, suburbs, the urban core, vast ranches, and about a dozen creeks and gulches. The High Line Canal Conservancy works with the Trail's eleven jurisdictions and the Canal's owner, Denver Water, to successfully create wonderful hiking and biking experiences throughout its entire length.

The Sand Creek Trail.

toilet on your right. Enjoy views up the Sand Creek as you continue on the trail.

Again, you'll cross Airport Road, but farther north on Airport than your first crossing. Continue your amble. Norfolk Glen will now be on your left. You'll eventually pass the sign to turn onto the High Line Canal Connector, and you'll be back at the beginning of the trail. Remember to take a right on the dirt trail that takes you back to the Morrison Nature Center.

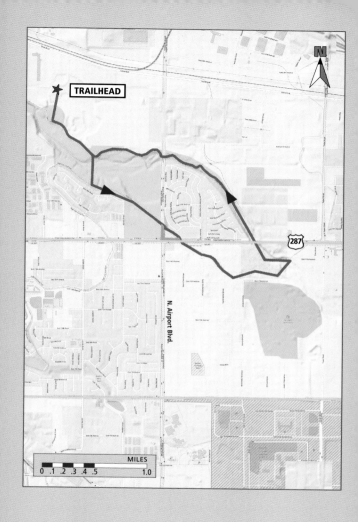

TRAILHEAD

N. Airport Blvd.

287

MILES
0 .1 .2 .3 .4 .5   1.0

AURORA:
NORFOLK GLEN LOOP

4. Aurora: Piney Creek Out-n-Back

RATING	Easy
DISTANCE	4.5 miles
TIME	1.5 hours
ELEVATION GAIN	Minimal
USAGE	Part of the regional trail system, you'll find walkers, bikers and joggers along this route.

COMMENTS: Cattails and cottonwoods. Rather than the trail name "Piney Creek," this trail should carry the name "Cattails and Cottonwoods." Making its way through the Piney Creek floodplain in the southeast corner of Aurora, this concrete trail invites a wonderful meander. Catch the gorgeous early fall color, the spread of both cottonwood and cattail snow puffs during the late fall, or the squawk of red-tailed hawks in the winter. Going almost a full 9 miles through Aurora, you'll pick the trail up just on the inside of the C-470 loop, making your way outside of the loop on the trail's southern end. Just when you think the trail is truly misnamed, you'll reach the end and eye a beautiful ridge of ponderosa pine spreading its evergreen image up to the east of the trail's end.

GETTING THERE: Larkspur Park is a residential park within the Saddle Rock Golf Club neighborhood. To get there, take E. Arapahoe Road all the way east, almost to the C-470 loop. Right before C-470, take a right on E. Easter Avenue. Take a right on S. Tibet Way. At the traffic circle, take a right and then another right, staying on E. Plymouth Circle. You'll see Larkspur Park at 22551 E. Plymouth Circle, Aurora, on your right and a few visitor parking spots on the left. Park here across from the park.

THE ROUTE: Once you've parked, find the trailhead at the north end of the park. Take a right on the trail, walking past the park, its playground and its restrooms on the way to C-470 after passing under Gartrell Road. Once you clear the C-470 under-pass, the trail opens up into a wide floodplain. Although houses and condos frame the basin, you'll quickly find the neighborhood noise fading away to the barks of prairie dogs.

You'll be in the Red-tailed Hawk Park. Watch, of course, for the flight of these majestic birds and identify them by their red tail feathers and white-fringed wings. They'll have the company of several other hawks and maybe even a falcon, eagle, or owl. With an abundance of prairie dogs, keep your eye out for many of their predators.

Eventually, you'll cross under Aurora Parkway. The basin becomes much more narrow, and you'll move along Piney Creek while the cottonwoods shade you. At a few points along the path, you can access the clear, shallow creek. Take a moment and listen to it pass you by. In about a mile, you'll start to notice pine trees appearing in the landscape. This is your sign that you're almost to the end of the trail.

The trail ends at the edge of the Tally'n Ranch neighborhood. Before turning around, look up to your left. You'll see a gorgeous pine ridge within the Ponderosa Preserve. Aurora owns the preserve and this natural area is accessible by a naturalist-guided tour: 303.326.8445. Once you've had your fill of the pine view, turn around and head back the way you came.

When you pass back under Aurora Parkway, rather than veering to the left, take a detour to the right. You'll continue up the slight hill and toward the playgrounds. Here, there are restrooms and water in case you're in need. Continue past the tot lots and the volleyball court until you come to a T in the trail. Take it right and head into more Aurora neighborhood. Or, to stay on this route, take a left. In a few hundred feet, you'll see a pebble trail to the right. Take the pebble trail and come across a secret, elevated trail through the wetlands.

The Piney Creek Trail.

Follow this curved bridge through the cattails until you come to the concrete trail. Take a right and then another right, and you'll be back on the Piney Creek Trail that you followed earlier. Continue back whence you came under C-470 and Gartell until you reach Larkspur.

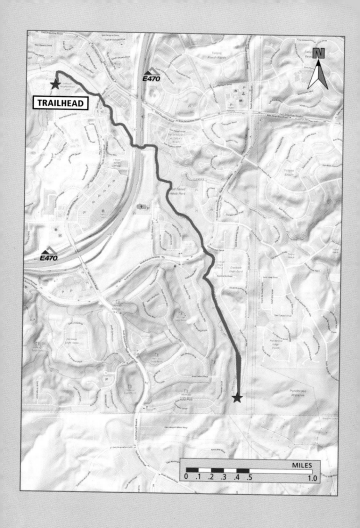

TRAILHEAD

E470

E470

MILES
0 .1 .2 .3 .4 .5 ⎯⎯⎯ 1.0

AURORA:
PINEY CREEK OUT-N-BACK

5. Brighton: Adams County Open Space

RATING	Easy
DISTANCE	4.5 miles
TIME	1.5 hours
ELEVATION GAIN	Minimal
USAGE	Part of the regional trail system, you'll find walkers, bikers and joggers along this route.

COMMENTS: Out in Adams County, just south of C-470 and mixed in with industrial use, hides a wonderful getaway tucked up next to the Platte River. In this open space sits a golf course, a disc golf course, a nature preserve, and lakes for fishing. Wrapping around these recreational resources, a trail circles and joins up with the Platte River Trail.

GETTING THERE: Take I-25 to I-76 toward Brighton. Continue on County Road 85 to E. 124th Avenue. Take a right on Park Boulevard to 9755 Henderson Rd., Brighton. Follow the signs to the nature preserve, parking near the restrooms at the trailhead on the south end of the parking lot.

THE ROUTE: The trailhead sign is just to the left of the informational signs across from the bathrooms next to the lake. Step onto the pebble trail and then take a sharp left, heading north along the lake. Veer to the left to go through the gate toward the nature preserve. You'll have a golf course tee on your left. Follow the dirt road around to the right, and then you'll see the tee for a disc golf course. This is the beginning of the preserve as well. If you want to make this loop even

The Platte River.

longer, veer to the left up into the preserve. Otherwise, follow the path around to the right onto a cement trail over another disc golf fairway.

You'll come around the backside of the lake from where you started. Continue along the concrete path and soon you'll come across unexpected views of the Platte River on your left. You're now on the Platte River Trail. Continue along the trail past the lake, and you'll have the choice to go right, staying within the park, or go to the left along the Platte River.

Go to the left under E. 124th Avenue, and journey along the Platte River for a little over 1.0 mile. Cottonwood trees provide some shade, and views to the east continue of the Platte River while the Rockies remain to your right. The trail continues, making large, sloping lefts and then rights, following the curve of the river. Walk along the river until you reach the tunnel at

Don't overlook the great urban hiking in north metro Denver.

E. 120th Parkway. At this point, you will have walked about 2.25 miles total. You can continue south of the Parkway along the Platte River Trail all the way to south Denver, if you'd like.

Or, turn around and head back toward the park. Once you pass back under E. 120th Avenue, turn left along the pebble trail into the parking lot. Continue through the parking lot, picking up the soft surface trail as it continues around the lake and across several pedestrian bridges. Notice flocks of white pelicans on the peninsula jutting out into the lake. The trail continues through the park past picnic tables and benches until arriving back at the parking lot where you started next to the preserve entrance.

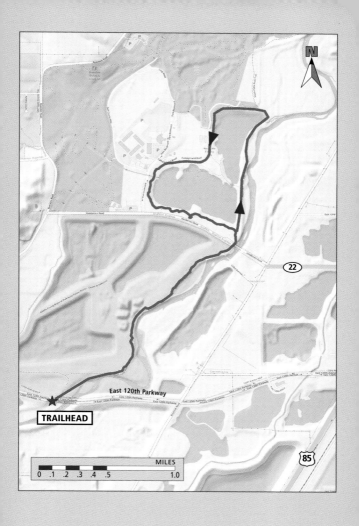

TRAILHEAD

East 120th Parkway

MILES
0   .1   .2   .3   .4   .5   1.0

6. Broomfield: Broomfield Open Space at Tom Frost Reservoir

RATING	Easy
DISTANCE	2 miles
TIME	45 minutes
ELEVATION GAIN	Minimal
USAGE	Part of the regional trail system, you'll find walkers, bikers and joggers along this route.

COMMENTS: The City of Broomfield has many open spaces, and all are inviting for a casual stroll. There's a Broomfield 100 challenge where you complete 100 miles in the Broomfield Open Space and record your accomplishments in a passport. Find that info on the City of Broomfield website. You can start your 100 miles on this sweet loop trail that circles the small Tom Frost Reservoir while having constant views of the mountains to the west.

GETTING THERE: Take I-25 north to West 128th Avenue in Broomfield. West 128th Avenue turns into E. Midway Boulevard. Go west to Lowell Street and take a right (north). There's a trailhead at that intersection, or go to the Paul Derda Rec Center, 13201 Lowell Blvd., Broomfield, up on the left. Park and head around the back of the rec center to the trail.

THE ROUTE: This is a simple loop route of about 2.0 miles. The crusher-fine trail loops around the Tom Frost Reservoir. Head north (to the right) and then the trail will veer to the left toward the mountains. It's an easy loop to follow, and there are a few shortcuts throughout the field. If you stay to the right,

In Broomfield, there's always a Rockies view.

you'll continue around the perimeter, eventually cutting to the left and then moving south along the neighborhood. The views across the watershed are spectacular as the marsh grasses and cattails pick up the season's hues, contrasting against the vast mountain range in the west.

The northern portion of the trail abuts the Broomfield Sports Fields where you can catch a pick-up game of soccer. Or, continue to the west, and you'll come across the other reservoir in this open space—Le Gault. Both of these small reservoirs are well stocked in case you brought along your

Everywhere in Denver, great urban hikes are just a few minutes away.

fishing pole. As you loop back along the southern edge of this open space, you'll pass a clam shell–shaped bench where you can sit and enjoy the lush colors of the marsh grasses and watch for migratory birds before heading back to the trail head.

A special thank you to Lisa Pardon at Walk2Connect for sharing this walk.

BROOMFIELD:
BROOMFIELD OPEN SPACE AT TOM FROST RESERVOIR

7. Centennial: South Suburban Horseshoe along the High Line Canal

RATING	Easy
DISTANCE	6 miles
TIME	3 hours
ELEVATION GAIN	Minimal
USAGE	Part of the regional trail system, you'll find walkers, bikers and joggers along this route. When on the High Line Canal, you may encounter horses which have the right of way.

COMMENTS: Walking along the High Line Canal Trail always grabs the imagination due to its 71-mile length. Where does it go, what does it connect? With the Denver Regional Trail System, the High Line Canal Trail, even with its twists and turns, backbones the entire system, connecting many other trails. In this route, you have the opportunity to walk a horseshoe shape and check off three of the regional trails while also getting some of the best views in Denver.

GETTING THERE: The route starts in Cherry Knolls Park, which you can approach from many different places. For this route, park along E. Easter Avenue at S. Knolls Way. Take I-25 to E. Arapahoe Road. Go west to S. University Boulevard. Go left on E. Easter Avenue and drive about 0.5 mile. You'll see Cherry Knolls Park on your left. Park along the street at 7077 S Elizabeth St, Centennial, CO, and access the park through the ramp down to the playground or many other places near the street where you park.

The High Line Canal.

THE ROUTE: Once you've found yourself in Cherry Knolls Park, cross Dry Creek and get onto the Dry Creek Trail and head north. You'll pass soccer fields on your right and quickly pass under Arapahoe Road and then again under University Boulevard.

Once you come out of the tunnel at University, you'll intersect with the High Line Canal. Take it left and you can walk to Waterton Canyon. But for this route, go right. Tennis courts and a portable toilet will be on the left. You'll cross over the High Line Canal and then veer to the left past the restroom building, with a parking lot on your right. Cross the road at the entrance to Goodsen Rec Center and continue going north. You'll immediately see the High Line Canal mile marker 25 on your left.

While on the High Line for the next 4 miles, you'll slowly walk in a horseshoe shape almost doubling back on yourself. The Rockies will be to your left for half of this walk and wide, vast montane views greet eager eyes. The soft surface trail invites many cyclists, walkers, joggers, and rollers, so keep to your right and mind your yields. The canal will always be on your right as well. If the canal is dry, you're welcome to actually walk in its bottom, grabbing some cooler temps if it's a warm, summer day.

Right about mile marker 25.5, you'll catch some of the best views the canal has to offer, including a nice place to sit on an old wheel wagon bench. After marker 26, cross over Josephine Way, Orchard, and Green Oaks Drive, which are all small, quaint crossings deep in the heart of Greenwood Village. Pass

Although Fall is a great time to urban hike in Denver, all seasons have their benefits.

mile marker 27. Soon an exercise station will be on your left and then the trail will make a big sweeping turn to the right, and you'll start heading southeasterly. Cross Franklin and under University again.

As you emerge out of the University tunnel, you might catch glimpses of Denver Tech Center. Journey along past the large red barns and ranchettes, crossing into Centennial. Just after you pass the High Line Canal sign welcoming you to Centennial, keep your eyes peeled for a large cottonwood snag on the right. Nailed to it is a flock of handmade, ceramic birds waiting for you to admire.

Always watch for coyotes and mind your dog leashes!

You'll pass mile marker 29, cross over Little Dry Creek, and you'll see a sign pointing to the Centennial Link Trail to the right. Some maps show this trail to be the end of the Little Dry Creek Trail. Either way, take the Centennial Link Trail off of the High Line and to the right. You'll immediately cross over Little Dry Creek onto a crusher-fine trail and then go under a bridge. At the first pedestrian bridge veering to the left, you will veer to the right and follow the trail's sweep upwardly to the right. You will see signs that say Little Dry Creek Trail.

Cross Colorado Boulevard. Shortly after this crossing, you'll come to a T in the trail. If you go to the right, you'll be back on the Centennial Link Trail. Rather, go straight and parallel the creek. On your left, you won't be able to miss the three-story tree house. Continue along the trail for another 0.5 mile next to the creek until you reach the end of the route at Heritage Village Park, where there is a nice parking lot and shelter. At this point, either turn around and walk back, or hail a Lyft or Uber to get back to your car.

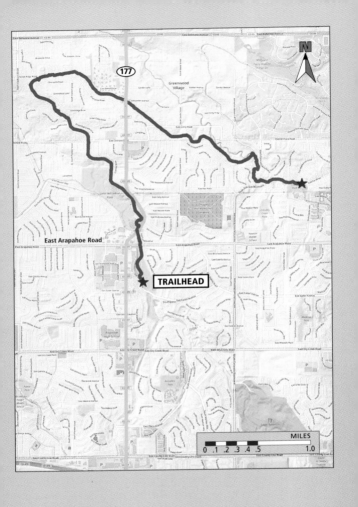

CENTENNIAL:
SOUTH SUBURBAN HORSESHOE ALONG THE HIGH LINE CANAL

8. Commerce City: Second Creek Loop

RATING	Easy
DISTANCE	3.7 miles
TIME	1 hour 45 minutes
ELEVATION GAIN	Minimal
USAGE	Part of the regional trail system, you'll find walkers, bikers and joggers along this route.

COMMENTS: This flat loop trail wrapping around Second Creek in the bellows of the prairie offers up super birds of prey bird watching. Although there are not many features to the landscape, this walk invites a good winter stroll. You'll want to keep a keen eye for small mammals making their way through winter while avoiding the coyote and birds of prey predators. The Second Creek Trail is an important trail in the future of trail connection in the northern parts of Denver. Plans are afoot to use the Second Creek Trail to connect the Rocky Mountain Arsenal Wildlife Refuge to the Two Lakes Refuge and the Rocky Flats Refuge. So although this trail sits alone in Commerce City, its future is as a major connector for parts afar. From its southern end, you can go under E. 96th Avenue and connect now to the Rocky Mountain Arsenal Wildlife Refuge's Perimeter Trail.

need caption

The Second Creek Trail.

GETTING THERE: Take I-70 to Quebec Street and go north. Merge to the right on Colorado Boulevard. Go right on E 96th Ave, then take a left on Chambers. Take a right on E. 104th Avenue and a left on Kittridge Street. The trailhead is half a block north on Kittridge on the left side near the Intersection of Kittridge St. and E. 104th Ave., Commerce City.

THE ROUTE: From the parking lot, head north about 0.25 mile and take a sharp left. You'll cross over a small footbridge and begin walking to the south. Pass under the giant Commerce City bridge at E. 104th Avenue. Continue along the pebble trail until reaching the fork at the bathrooms. Stay to the right before passing the bathrooms. You'll be on a loop through the Buckley Ranch Open Space.

Before reaching the bridge at E. 96th Avenue, turn left and loop back toward the north. At the restrooms, you'll join back up to where you split off the fork. Continue north under the E. 104th Avenue bridge. At the picnic tables, take a right. You'll loop to the south on the east side of the creek and then loop back north to the parking lot.

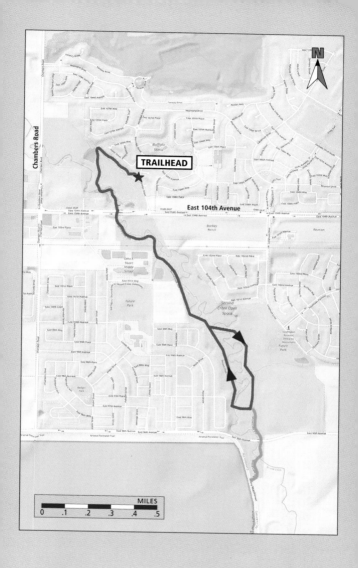

Denver: 9 Creeks Loop

The Denver Regional Trail System has hundreds of miles of trails covering many counties and areas of Colorado's Front Range. The 9 Creeks Loop traverses four of Denver's Regional Trails, including the Sand Creek Trail, the High Line Canal, the Cherry Creek Trail, and the Platte River Trail. Drawing a nice circumference around the city of Denver, this 41-mile loop passes through urban, suburban, creeks, woods, and commercial areas, offering many views of Denver's 9 Creeks area. While walking this loop, you'll enjoy the watersheds and creeks of First Creek, Second Creek, Sand Creek, Lee Gulch, Cherry Creek, Dry Creek, Toll Gate Creek, High Line Canal, and the Platte River.

At 41 miles, the 9 Creeks Loop cannot be walked in one attempt. There is no camping allowed along any of the trails, so you must walk it in segments. The 9 Creeks Loop is broken up here into eight segments, each with its own trailhead. To follow this route, you'll walk one-way along the segment, stopping and starting at the subsequent trailheads. Although the walk starts at Globeville at the corner of 38th St. and Arkins Ct., Denver, you can really start at whichever trailhead makes sense to you. This route goes clockwise around Denver.

The 9 Creeks Loop gives you a 360 degree view of Denver.

DENVER:
9 CREEKS LOOP

9. Segment 1: Globeville Landing to Dahlia Trailhead

RATING	Easy
DISTANCE	~ 5 miles
TIME	~ 2 hours
ELEVATION GAIN	Minimal
USAGE	Part of the regional trail system, you'll find walkers, bikers and joggers along this route.

COMMENTS: Globeville sits north of Denver along the Platte River, railroad lines bisect it, and Interstates 70 and 25 eventually would run through it. Only one street car stop ever existed here, so, historically, due to the limited access to safe and fluid walking areas, the workers of the Globe Smelter stayed and felt isolated from Denver. In addition, the configuration of roads and the Interstate earned the area the nickname, "The Mousetrap," due to the impossibility of navigating the ons and offs of the major thoroughfares. But funny thing is, when walking along the Platte River Trail, it's pretty straightforward and easy to follow.

On this route, you'll see some of the best views of the Platte River as you pass through Globeville into Denver's water treatment areas (both historic and current), past its historic Riverfront Cemetery, cross over the confluence of the Platte River and then turn onto the Sand Creek Greenway into Commerce City. You'll get a glimpse at large petroleum and gas processing plants and start to understand the backstory to how Denver drinks water and transits. Finally, you'll exit this segment at the Dahlia Trailhead.

The historic Riverside Cemetery.

GETTING THERE: Take I-70 to Washington Street and go south. Take a left on Arkins Court. Park on the street next to Globeville Landing which is the corner of 38th St. and Arkins Ct., Denver.

THE ROUTE: Park at Globeville Landing and start the 9 Creeks Loop by going clockwise, or to the right. You'll be on the 8-foot wide concrete Platte River Trail. In no time, you'll arrive at Northside Park, or what used to be the old Denver sewage plant, which closed in the '80s. After becoming destitute and an eyesore, the city, with the help of the National Guard, cleaned up the brown field and turned it into a park. Take a moment to read the interpretation of the park and use the restrooms.

Up ahead, you'll cross the Burlington Ditch. Created in the 1880s by a group of enterprisers who wanted to sell water rights and construction bonds, the Burlington Ditch flows into Barr Lake. Next to the ditch, some of Denver's elite

The Sand Creek Trail's northern end.

are buried at Riverside Cemetery. It continues to offer space now as does the Fairmount Cemetery to the south.

You may smell the wastewater plant about 0.5 mile before approaching it, so it's best to do this segment when it's cooler and the wind blows to the north or west. Pass the brown-colored buildings and holding tanks as you make your way to the bridge crossing the river at the confluence with the Sand Creek Trail. If you continue north on the Platte River Trail, you'll end up in Thornton. Rather, cross the river and end up on the Sand Creek Greenway.

Looking over the edge of the bridge, gawk at the 4–6-foot long catfish in the effluent. Immediately after exiting the bridge, the trail turns southeast, and you'll promptly cross the Burlington Ditch again, approaching the Suncor petroleum plant.

The Sand Creek Trail abuts closely to the edge of the Sand Creek, and large marshlands house wonderful birding along the trail. Continue along, going under caged areas that protect you from falling debris from train tracks.

Soon you'll pass under Vasquez Boulevard, arriving at the Dahlia Trailhead, the end of segment 1 and the beginning of segment 2.

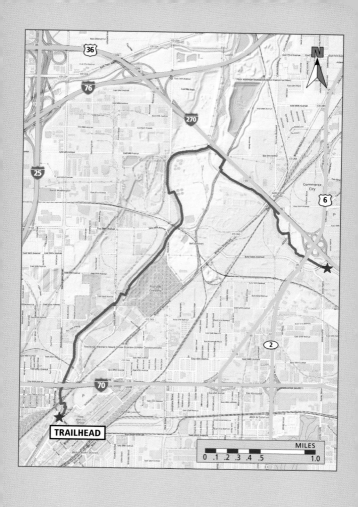

SEGMENT 1:
GLOBEVILLE LANDING TO DAHLIA TRAILHEAD

10. Segment 2: Dahlia Trailhead to Bluff Lake Nature Center Trailhead

RATING	Easy
DISTANCE	~ 5 miles
TIME	~ 2 hours
ELEVATION GAIN	Minimal
USAGE	Part of the regional trail system, you'll find walkers, bikers and joggers along this route.

COMMENTS: On this second segment, the underpinning story is one of transportation. You'll be walking through where the old Stapleton Airport was, now replaced by the new urban-infill Stapleton neighborhood. But despite the growth of residences and the supporting businesses, this area along the Sand Creek was first developed as a transit zone. You'll see the impact of I-25, I-70, I-270, and I-76 all coming together along with the trains and supporting road systems, as this area was once the major distribution point for western commerce. Some might argue that it still is. Nonetheless, you'll quickly leave the hustle and bustle of transit's heartbeat and end up passing urban farms and preserves on your way to Bluff Lake Nature Center.

GETTING THERE: Take I-70 to Washington Street and go north. Turn right on 47th Street. Turn left on 44th Street/E. 46th Avenue, then left on Vasquez Boulevard. Turn right on E. 56th Avenue, then right on Sand Creek. Turn into parking lot at 4900 Sandcreek Dr. S., Commerce City on your right.

Along the Sand Creek Trail, you'll see remnants of the old Stapleton airport's runways.

THE ROUTE: Hop back on the Sand Creek Trail at the Dahlia Trailhead and go left, or east. You'll walk mostly a straight route along Sand Creek with I-270 on your left. Due to the interesting rock retaining wall, you'll barely notice the Interstate. Focus on the creek and its wildlife as you make your way under some overpasses and train trestles.

You'll cross over Sand Creek and going to your left, make a large loop under Quebec Street. At the T in the trail, stay to your left, going under I-70 and then crossing the pedestrian bridge. At this point, the trail turns to pebble trail and makes a Z-shape on the way to Central Park Boulevard. Cross under Central Park Boulevard on the new concrete trail.

Once you make your way under Central Park Boulevard and back along the creek, you'll settle into a nice straight walk for about 1.0 mile. Sand Creek will be on your right. After about 0.5 mile you'll notice concrete walls along the banks of the waterway. At one time, the Stapleton Airport runways crossed here on a bridge built for the airplanes. You can find old pictures of planes taxiing on a bridge—it was here.

After passing through the old runways, you'll continue along and come to the Sand Creek Trailhead off of Smith Road. On the left you'll see a large parking lot, a bench, and a portable toilet. There is some interpretation of the fauna for the area. After taking a break, continue east along the trail. To the south, you'll start to see Stapleton housing and then you'll come across Stapleton's Central Park.

The Stapleton neighborhood is the ingenuousness of an urban redesign. In 1995, the Stapleton Airport closed due to noise and size, and the Denver International Airport was built about 15 miles north. Forest City won the rights to redevelop the old airport into a community designed for walking, green spaces, and families. The south side of Stapleton has about 15,000 homes, and the Northfield area, on the north side of I-70, will have as many homes. The Sand Creek Trail runs through most of Stapleton.

You'll approach Havana and be a bit at a loss for how to get across the creek and continue on the trail. You'll need to go up to Havana and cross on the sidewalk bridge to the south. Continue along the street until you get to the intersection with the light. You'll see apartments on your right. Cross the street, then continue on the Sand Creek Trail to the right. Don't be fooled by going to the left, as the trail does not follow the Creek here. Continue along the trail as it runs parallel to the road with Bluff Lake on your left and the road on your right. Prairie dogs will probably bark directions to you as you walk by.

You'll arrive at the end of 9 Creeks Loop segment 2, Bluff Lake Nature Center. A local getaway, this quaint reserve not only has a nice place to take a break and use a portable toilet, but if you have time and interest, you can definitely take the steps down into the reserve and explore the local flora and fauna. Check the center's calendar for seasonal events. An interesting note about the nature center—when it was being built, they used the old runway concrete from Stapleton Airport. Volunteers called the rock "Staple-Rock."

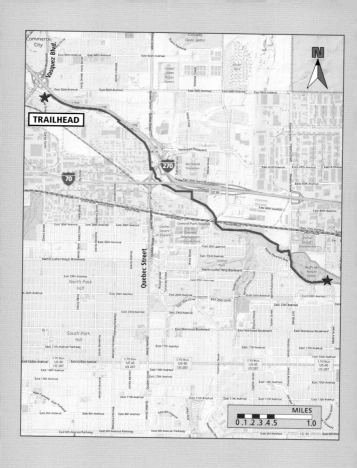

11. Segment 3: Bluff Lake Nature Center Trailhead to Hinkley High School

RATING	Easy
DISTANCE	~ 5 miles
TIME	~ 2 hours
ELEVATION GAIN	Minimal
USAGE	Part of the regional trail system, you'll find walkers, bikers and joggers along this route.

COMMENTS: This segment introduces you to Aurora. After leaving the city of Denver, you'll wander through the outskirts of Aurora and venture into one of its original party places, the Star K Ranch. You'll jump off the Sand Creek Trail and join the High Line Canal Trail, making your way through rural areas of Aurora, seeing goats, sheep, chickens, and maybe even a remote-control car track. The High Line Canal will stay with you, running parallel to the trail, until you get back to the city of Denver.

GETTING THERE: Take I-70 to Havana Street and go south. Take a left on E. 29th Drive. The nature center, 3400 Havana Way, Denver, will be on your left.

THE ROUTE: After taking a break at the center, continue along the trail. About 100 yards east of the nature center, the trail leaves the road and ducks into the nature center property. Shortly, you'll cross into Aurora on the Sand Creek Trail. The City of Aurora has created a nice underpass crossing where you'll go under the new light rail tracks into Aurora and then under Peoria. Just to the east of Peoria is a footbridge that crosses over Sand Creek again.

The first part of the trail in Aurora continues on pebble trail and runs parallel to Sand Creek. Residences frame both sides of the trail, and the Sand Creek Greenway has done a nice job with signage. The trail is flat and easy to follow. Shortly, the trail becomes concrete at about 30th Avenue in Aurora. The creek parallels down the bank to the south.

Cross over Sable and continue along the backside of a concrete plant. The trail dips down into some woods and along Sand Creek. Look for evidence of beavers! Several trees have been gnawed and felled. Shortly, you'll reach the entrance of Star K Ranch.

Star K Ranch, settled by Virgil "Pop" Stark a half century ago when he was forced off where the Rocky Mountain Army Arsenal decided to appear, became the destination for parties for Pop's retirement. Over 3000 guests would converge for 3-day parties, enjoying the great outdoors of the ranch, its wildlife and its wonderful view. On the Star K Ranch is the Morrison Center, which includes parts of Pop's home and nature exhibits.

Continue east down the trail and in about 0.5 mile you'll see a sign that says, "High Line Canal 1/2 Mile." Take a right, venture down through the woods, across Sand Creek and up to the High Line Canal. Take a right. You'll now be on the High Line Canal Trail, which runs all the way from Green Valley Ranch to the north down to Waterton Canyon to the south. For the 9 Creeks Loop, you'll stay on the High Line for about 10 miles.

The High Line Canal Trail offers up a nice 8-foot-wide cement path. Notice the High Line Canal mile markers, which will entertain you until you get to Cherry Creek. Cross over Colfax at the crosswalk and continue into Aurora. The City of Aurora, one of the fastest growing cities in Colorado, was once named Fletcher after the original founder, Donald Fletcher. He garnered the water rights for the town and began

Star K Ranch is not to be missed.

building a subdivision full of what was known as "Fletcher homes." You can still find a few Fletcher homes north of Colfax between Havana and Peoria. But when the silver bust broke up Denver and its environs, Fletcher fled with his water rights. The remaining citizens renamed the town, Aurora. Fortunately for them, the High Line Canal was being built, and it brought water out to the farms and agriculture all the way east of Denver here in Aurora.

Thus, when walking in Aurora, you'll often stumble upon unexpected farms and ranches squeezed in between new residences. In this mile along the High Line Canal, you'll find goat, sheep, and chicken farms. Also in this same area, you might see a remote-control track called, "Bang Town" in someone's backyard across from the sheep farm.

Moving along and past the farms, the trail continues behind Hinkley High School. Hinkley has one of the few public school pools and a wonderful football/track field. On the other side of the canal, the fields continue, including soccer and baseball fields. Here, in the parking lot of Hinkley High School, is the end of segment 3.

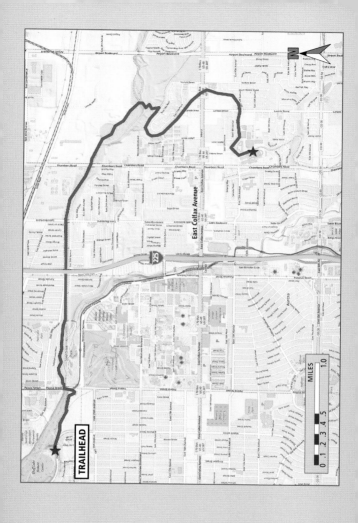

TRAILHEAD

East Colfax Avenue

MILES

0 .1 .2 .3 .4 .5   1.0

12. Segment 4: Hinkley High School to Del Mar Elwood Park

RATING	Easy
DISTANCE	~ 5 miles
TIME	~ 2 hours
ELEVATION GAIN	Minimal
USAGE	Part of the regional trail system, you'll find walkers, bikers and joggers along this route.

COMMENTS: The route takes you through one of the best and most historic areas of Aurora, DeLaney Farms. Once a major homestead and vegetable farm of the area, now DeLaney Farms plays host to Denver Urban Garden's CSA program, an apiary, and several rookeries.

GETTING THERE: Take I-225 to the Colfax exit and go east. Take a left on Chambers, then another left into Hinkley High School parking lot, 1250 Chambers Rd., Aurora. The trail runs behind the football field.

THE ROUTE: Return to the trail behind Hinkley High School and continue south to the right. You'll parallel Chambers Street and soon come to DeLaney Farms on your right and Community College of Aurora on your left. The college anchors along the canal, and you'll see the college's observatory. The observatory is open to the public on certain nights, so be sure to check their schedule if there's a particular celestial event happening that you want to see.

After passing the college, set your sights on observing the wonderful DeLaney Farms. Settled in the late 1800s, DeLaney

Aurora has great urban hiking options.

Farms now spans 168 acres and is managed by Denver Urban Gardens. The DUG runs a CSA where anyone can buy a membership and get fresh fruits and veggies throughout the season and/or exchange work for products. While walking here, you'll see hundreds of prairie dogs, hawks, foxes, deer and rabbits. It's a great location to really amble along and enjoy the scenery.

Just before actually reaching the barns of the historic farm, you'll cross over two of the nine creeks—the West Toll Gate and the Toll Gate. At the crossing there's a great view of the locks along the canal that control the water flow through Aurora and down along the Toll Gate. In addition, the trail continues by the historic buildings of DeLaney, including the last of two remaining round, wooden, short silos. Here, you can also see where tours for the farm start from, including tours of the

Some folks have landscaped their backyards to embrace the trails running behind them.

apiary, the silo, and the homestead. Finally, the trail goes under Chambers via the Weddig Tunnel, which houses some really interesting stainless steel artwork.

Come out of the tunnel, passing the Aurora Government Center on your left and High Line Canal mile marker 54. In just a short distance, cross over Sable Avenue, which is poorly marked for cars looking for pedestrians. Aurora Town Center, which hosts a Target and many shops, restaurants, and vendors, will be on your left.

The trail continues west under I-225. Follow any detour signs to get on the west side of I-225. The trail follows the Aurora Golf Course. Many of the homes on the north side of the trail connect their yards to the trail with nice landscaping and walkways to their backyard fences.

At Peoria Street, take a right off the trail and head north half a block. Here you'll end segment 3 at Del Mar Elwood Park. Note the bathrooms just to the north near the parking lots.

TRAILHEAD

MILES

SEGMENT 4:
HINKLEY HIGH SCHOOL TO DEL MAR ELWOOD PARK

13. Segment 5: Del Mar Elwood Park to Eloise May Library

RATING	Easy
DISTANCE	~ 5 miles
TIME	~ 2 hours
ELEVATION GAIN	Minimal
USAGE	Part of the regional trail system, you'll find walkers, bikers and joggers along this route.

COMMENTS: With lots of variety on this segment, you'll cross from Aurora into Denver. From very urban to the lovely Windsor Gardens, you'll see evidence of the mosaic that the trail makes as it ventures through all of Denver proper and ending just beyond Fairmount Cemetery, Denver's second oldest yet most famous cemetery.

GETTING THERE: Take I-225 to E 6th Avenue and go west. Take a left on Del Mar Circle at 12000 E. 6th Ave., Aurora. Park near the southern end of the park.

THE ROUTE: Head south out of Del Mar Park on Peoria about half a block to the High Line Canal and take a right. In no time, you'll arrive at Expo Park. Along Alameda at the entry to Expo Park, there is an historic sign for the High Line Canal and then a small sign from the city of Aurora that says "Trail" with an arrow. The "Trail" sign goes to the Westerly Creek Trail through Expo Park. The High Line Canal Trail is the pebble trail on the right, which parallels Westerly Creek and then veers off to the right, or west. That's the one to take, and you can also add another creek to your nine, the Westerly Creek.

The pump house at Fairmount Cemetery along the High Line Canal.

The pebble trail continues along to High Line Canal mile marker 50, and then you'll cross Havana and back into the city of Denver. The loop moves westerly for quite some time, and you'll finally view mountains in the distance. Continue along the loop, which turns from pebble to asphalt to concrete. As the loop becomes more populous, so does the vegetation. Soon beautiful varieties of trees will shade you as you amble along, and you'll certainly notice that water must have flown through the canal much more recently.

In no time, you'll come along the part of the High Line Canal Trail that goes behind Windsor Gardens. This active senior living community brings out many folks to the loop. Continue along for about 0.5 mile to the pump house and back entry into Fairmount Cemetery. Here, Denver Water services its most northern and largest customer, Fairmount Cemetery, from the High Line Canal. A pump house sits along the canal and pipes water into the cemetery, where beautiful landscaping and treescapes greet visitors. Several champion trees and one of the largest heritage rose collections in North America grow here. Reinhard Schuetze, father of Denver's park design, designed this cemetery. But not only are the buildings and landscaping awe-striking, so are many of the tombstones. Take a break and enjoy some of the cemetery art before heading down the trail.

Once you've enjoyed Fairmount, move on down the asphalt path, reaching the intersection of Parker and Mississippi. Take extreme caution when crossing this intersection and use the crosswalk and its buttons. Eventually, the High Line Canal Conservancy plans to put a tunnel under this intersection. In the meantime, cross carefully. Follow the trail until reaching Florida Avenue.

At Florida, instead of continuing along the trail, take a left on Florida and walk about 1,000 feet to your trail-end at the Eloise May Library on your left.

TRAILHEAD

N

East Alameda Avenue

East Mississippi Avenue

MILES
0 .1 .2 .3 .4 .5   1.0

SEGMENT 5:
DEL MAR ELWOOD PARK TO ELOISE MAY LIBRARY

14. Segment 6: Eloise May Library to Garland Park

RATING	Easy
DISTANCE	~ 5 miles
TIME	~ 2 hours
ELEVATION GAIN	Minimal
USAGE	Part of the regional trail system, you'll find walkers, bikers and joggers along this route.

COMMENTS: After walking on the High Line, you'll finally exit the High Line Canal Trail and start the Cherry Creek Trail. The atmosphere changes from a meander to a commute! The Cherry Creek Golf Course homes dot the horizon along the golf course as you head northwest up the creek and into downtown Denver.

GETTING THERE: Take I-25 to E. Evans Avenue and go east. Take a left on Quebec Street, then a right on Florida Avenue. Park in the western edge of the library parking lot, 1471 S. Parker Rd., Denver, on the north side of Florida Avenue.

THE ROUTE: Park at Eloise May Library, and then walk 1,000 feet to the west along Florida to pick up the trail. Take a left and continue south. The trail will be double-wide at this point, with bikers taking the asphalt and walkers taking the pebble trail that parallels it. Head under Iliff through the tunnel, and you'll come out at the Cherry Creek Golf Course.

The asphalt trail parallels the golf course with nice vistas of giant houses on the right and nicely appointed apartments on the left. The users of the trail change here, being replaced by

You're always near a creek on the 9 Creeks Loop.

folks who are serious about their exercise: walkers, runners, and bicyclists alike!

After walking next to the Cherry Creek fairways, you'll come across a large, odd, cement structure on your left. The High Line Canal diverts through this structure under Cherry Creek to the south. Right past the structure, Cherry Creek offers up a cool respite of flowing water, trees, and even a bench. Signage directs you south on the High Line Canal Trail or west to the Cherry Creek North Trail. Head to the right along the Cherry Creek Trail and pick up the next of the 9 Creeks—Cherry Creek.

Be sure to stay to the right and share the trail.

Immediately, Cherry Creek's atmosphere changes. Where the High Line sports casual walkers and evening strollers, the Cherry Creek Trail becomes a raceway, especially during rush hour. Mind yourself and stay to the right of the trail or use the dirt footpath that parallels it. You'll eventually leave the Cherry Creek Golf Course, cross over Cherry Creek, and into an industrial area. The golf course to your right is replaced by a chain link fence.

While wandering through the industrial area, you'll come across your next creek of nine, the Goldsmith Gulch (whose creek is also known as Goldsmith Gulch) at Cook Park. Cross over Monaco and continue along until you come to Garland Park, your stop for this segment. Another busy park, pay attention to the large amount of running and biking traffic as you finish this particular segment of the 9 Creeks Loop.

TRAILHEAD

83

East Iliff Avenue

MILES
0   .25   .5   .75   1.0

15. Segment 7: Garland Park to Sunken Gardens Park

RATING	Easy
DISTANCE	~ 5 miles
TIME	~ 2 hours
ELEVATION GAIN	Minimal
USAGE	Part of the regional trail system, you'll find walkers, bikers and joggers along this route.

COMMENTS: If you're a fan of the Cherry Creek area, you'll love this segment of the trail. Taking you from 4 Mile Historic Park to the mall to the industrial area and out, you'll experience Cherry Creek from a pedestrian view—one that many don't get a chance to enjoy.

GETTING THERE: Take Colorado Boulevard to E. Mississippi Avenue and go east. Take a right on Cherry Creek S. Drive. Take a left on S. Holly Street then a right on Cherry Creek N. Drive. Take a left into Garland Park and park near 6300 E Mississippi Ave., Denver, as close as possible to the Cherry Creek Trail.

THE ROUTE: Jump back on the trail from Garland Park and head to the right, or north. You'll still be walking along the creek. Shortly you'll pass 4 Mile Historic Park, a historical property that recreates life on the prairie in the 1800s. Imagine yourself homesteading and farming as you continue north along Cherry Creek. Here the bicycles pick up pretty quickly, so stay to the right of the trail along the dirt path paralleling the trail.

Picnicking on Cherry Creek.

The creek remains on your left while multi-story business buildings decorate the road to the right. Smaller parks sneak their way in between the buildings, offering some respite and bathrooms. Soon, high-rise residences begin to appear, and you'll stumble upon the City of Takayama Park, a Denver sister city. The City of Takayama Park, the second park in Denver's Sister Cities program, honors the beauty and relationship between the two cities that share commonalities in mountains, rivers, hot springs, and industry. The park houses beautiful bonsai trees and respite from the business of the Cherry Creek Trail.

Continue along Cherry Creek Trail, named after the choke-cherries along its bank, and you'll come across the next Denver Sister City, the City of Karmiel Park. Sharing a love for community, these two sister cities have developed their relationship through live readings about the Holocaust, sharing textbooks and musical instruments, and inviting students to visit. This fourth of ten Denver Sister Cities continues to bring love and kindness through a variety of global events each year.

Not long after, you'll come to the Cherry Creek Mall. Denver's posh shopping district attracts regionally from around the West. The trail actually diverts from the mall and goes across the creek through some wonderful views. It seems that bikers take this trail and walkers stay up along the mall. But the trail officially goes across the creek, so take the path that is most comfortable to you.

After you get past Cherry Creek Mall, the trail continues west along 1st Avenue. Rather than walking on the very narrow multi-use path along Denver Country Club, you may want to cross 1st Avenue and head up to 4th Avenue. Go west through the neighborhood along 4th until you reach Corona Street. Head south on Corona, crossing 1st and jump back on the Cherry Creek Trail. Walk to 8th Avenue, where you'll exit the trail to enter Sunken Gardens Park.

Several gulches empty into Cherry Creek.

16. Segment 8: Sunken Gardens Park to Globeville

RATING	Easy
DISTANCE	~ 5 miles
TIME	~ 2 hours
ELEVATION GAIN	Minimal
USAGE	Part of the regional trail system, you'll find walkers, bikers and joggers along this route.

COMMENTS: This segment, which completes the 9 Creek Loop, takes you through a walking art gallery. When you think you've had your fill of artistic beauty, you round the corner at Confluence Park and see the natural beauty of two water bodies colliding. You'll continue north along the Platte River, enjoying its wide views, finally reaching the end of the loop at Globeville.

GETTING THERE: Take I-25 to W. 6th Avenue and go east to Elati Street. Go north to W. 9th Avenue and turn right. Park in or near Sunken Gardens Park, 1099 Speer Blvd., Denver, as close to the east side as possible to access Cherry Creek Trail.

THE ROUTE: Return back to the trail by crossing over the creek and turning north on the east side of the creek, which is designated for walkers. Now that you're back on the trail, cement walls will surround you on both sides as the trail continues next to the creek. You'll discover one of Denver's best-kept secrets, its public art fund. This fund sets aside 1 percent of $1 million capital projects within the city for public art, and part of those funds go for street art. The cement walls became canvases for global street artists to share their craft. Changing

Art along Cherry Creek.

frequently, you'll see dozens of murals along the walls as you amble toward Confluence Park.

At the intersection of Cherry Creek and the Platte River sits Confluence Park. Overlooked by REI to the west, apartments to the northeast, and a park to the southeast, this Mecca of activity draws water lovers, outdoor enthusiasts, and sunbathers from around the region. Kayakers, tubers, sand castle builders, and coffee drinkers mingle here enjoying the exciting rapids

The Platte River.

and confluence of these two water bodies. On the cement walls bordering the water, artists have painted their best pieces.

Take a right at Platte River, picking up the ninth of the nine creeks, and enter the Platte River Trail. You'll go under 15th Street and meander through Commons Park as it links to City of Cuernavaca Park. These two urban parks invite all types of adventure and artwork. Get distracted and enjoy the parks or the cafes that front them, or continue down river (northward).

The South Platte River eventually flows to the Gulf of Mexico via the Mississippi by way of Nebraska. Its history roots in the Colorado gold rush, and it owns the birth of Denver along its banks. Like many rivers that flow through cities, it's been through its need for respect—from a place to dump trash, chemicals, and waste, to a place that residents love to fish and boat. Known for its Brown and Rainbow Trout, the river hosts many events and games throughout the year. Walking along the Platte always brings forth a variety of people and views.

The Platte River Trail, a concrete path 8 feet wide, follows the west side of the river for a short while and then crosses over to the east. Although people still use the Platte River Trail to commute, it's not nearly as busy as the Cherry Creek Trail. The Platte is also a corridor for historical wayfarers and new wayfarers alike. Jack Kerouac used the trail to journey from the Denargo Fruit Market to downtown to meet up with his buddies Neal Cassady and Alan Ginsberg. Currently, some of Denver's homeless hang along the Platte, spending their days awaiting their next moves. Don't let this discourage you, just be alert as you amble northward.

In about 1.0 mile, you'll arrive at Globeville, back where you started the 9 Creeks Loop. At this point, you will have crossed over nine bodies of water—Sand Creek, High Line Canal, Westerly Creek, Toll Gate, West Toll Gate, East Toll Gate, Cherry Creek, Goldsmith Gulch, and the Platte River—and covered about 41 miles.

TRAILHEAD

MILES

0   .25   .5   .75   1.0

SEGMENT 8:
SUNKEN GARDENS PARK TO GLOBEVILLE

Walking in City Park always brings great views and adventure.

17. Denver: City Park Loop

RATING	Easy
DISTANCE	2.5 miles
TIME	1 hour
ELEVATION GAIN	Minimal
USAGE	Part of the regional trail system, you'll find walkers, bikers and joggers along this route.

COMMENTS: The city of Denver takes great care of City Park, making almost all of its trails easily accessible all year round. Whether walking, skating, biking, snow shoeing, or cross country skiing, this park invites everyone to come outside daily. What's also nice is that this route can be longer or shorter; veer to the left at forks to make it shorter or veer to the right to make it longer.

GETTING THERE: From I70, take Colorado Boulevard south to Montview Boulevard. Turn right into the Denver Museum of Nature and Science, 2001 Colorado Blvd., Denver, and park.

If parking is full, find parking along 22nd Avenue or within the park. This route starts at the giant snow mastodon in the southwest corner of the parking lot.

THE ROUTE: Find the giant snow mastodon in the museum parking lot and look to the west toward the boathouse and lake. You'll see the famous view of this 320-acre park dating back to 1880, which now homes the Denver Zoo, the Museum of Nature and Science, 5 formal gardens, 3,500 trees of 40 different species, several monuments and statues, and three lakes.

Go down the stairs, pass the rose garden, and get on the loop—called the Mile High Loop—that circles the lake. Walk toward the boathouse, but instead of circling the lake, take the grand staircase down to the right. Veer to the right to the east of the canon and behind the zoo. Listen for animal sounds as you pass Duck Lake on your right and the back of the Martin Luther King, Jr. statue on your left.

Continue through the tennis courts. If you want to go farther, veer to the right and catch the perimeter trail, or continue straight and loop back through the tennis courts, heading back to the boathouse. Pass the formal gardens and the front of the MLK statue, veering to the right of the boathouse. After the boathouse, veer again to the right to pick up additional distance, or hug Ferril Lake, named after the poet laureate, until reaching its eastern point. Say hello to the Canadian geese that populate the park almost year round. Go back up the staircase at the water feature, which is on during the summer. You'll be back at the snow mastodon. If you have time, stop in the museum for some good hands-on science.

In the middle of City Park lies the Martin Luther King, Jr, memorial plaza. One of the most interesting monuments to MLK in the US, it also contains full-body replicas of Rosa Parks, Gandhi, Frederick Douglass, and Sojourner Truth. Be sure to see the bronze inlay of how slaves were shipped as cargo, and take a few moments to reflect on the four historic panels around the perimeter of the plaza. Towards the southwestern edge of the plaza is an interpretative panel with audio.

City Park has an interesting collection of statues. Here is the Scottish
poet Robert Burns, who has no connection to Colorado.

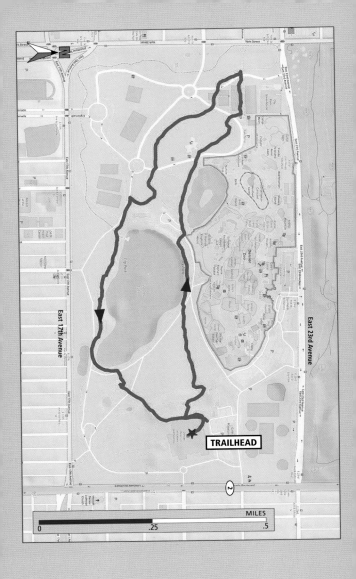

TRAILHEAD

MILES

0 .25 .5

DENVER:
CITY PARK LOOP

18. Denver: Confluence Park Clover

RATING	Easy
DISTANCE	3.5 miles
TIME	1.5 hours
ELEVATION GAIN	Minimal
USAGE	Part of the regional trail system, you'll find walkers, bikers and joggers along this route. This area is very busy with biking traffic, especially on the east side of the Platte River and the north side of the Cherry Creek, both of which you can avoid by walking on the west and south sides, respectively.

COMMENTS: Vibrancy calls for a great walk along the Platte River. There's always something going on at the confluence of the Platte River and Cherry Creek. Whether new installations of amazing wall art, a kayaking competition, walkers out for strolls or bikers whizzing by, this area at the intersection of Denver's two prominent rivers invites all walkers any time of the year. This route makes a wonderful 3-leaf clover pattern that you can extend or shorten. Go farther south on the Platte, farther east on the Cherry, or farther north on the Platte. If you're curious, just let your feet take you on a journey. This route will always be full of surprises.

GETTING THERE: Take I-25 to 23rd Avenue/20th Avenue exit. Turn right on 20th to Central Street and curve around to the left. Take a left on 15th Street then right on Platte Street. Look for 2-hour meter parking nearby, or REI offers two hours of free parking to customers.

When crossing the Platte, be sure to enjoy the views both up and down river.

THE ROUTE: Once you've parked in a 2-hour or more spot, walk behind REI. You'll see the Platte River and a footbridge. Instead of crossing the bridge, head south along the Platte River. The concrete trail takes you past Elitch Gardens, moved here from its historical site a few miles away at 38th and Tennyson, on your left. Enjoy the laughs and sounds coming from the roller coaster as you continue south along the path to Bronco Bridge. Notice the giant stadium to the right where the Denver Broncos play. Just past the auto bridge is a footbridge. Take that across the river and head north, paralleling the walk you just traveled on the west side of the river.

You'll return back to the confluence of the two rivers. Stay to your right and continue past the pedestrian bridge that crosses back to REI. Rather, go north, taking the sharp right turn onto Cherry Creek Trail. Immediately take the left across the creek on the brown pedestrian bridge. Cross Cherry Creek, then take the series of ramps to the left down to the creek. At the bottom of the ramp, turn left. You'll be on the north side of Cherry Creek Trail where pedestrians have access. The south side of the creek is for cyclists.

Enjoy the amazing street art along the walls abutting the creek. Changed annually, these works of art range from abstract multicolored adventures to whimsical characters. Art graces the walls of Cherry Creek for about 3 miles. If you choose, continue all the way past the Convention Center or beyond. For this particular walk, amble to the train trestle and turn around. When you reach the ramps to go back up across the pedestrian bridge from whence you came, instead continue around the bend in the river and find yourself walking north along the Platte River.

The South Platte River plays the protagonist in the story of Denver's growth. Here at this confluence, the city sprouted, putting its growth in the ability of the Platte to deliver good, clean snowmelt for safe, fresh water. But as with most cities, Denver underestimated its ability to keep the river clean and to quench its growing city's thirst. A series of dams now hold

The ever changing artwork along Cherry Creek at Confluence Park.

the Platte's water, and the river once again thrives as a recreational and commercial draw for Denver while also providing the Front Range with a vital water supply. Although this route only takes you a few miles along its banks, the South Platte continues flowing north and then east to Nebraska.

Continue your walk north along the Platte. The city of Denver will be on your right. You'll pass through Denver's Commons Park. If you want a bite to eat, walk a bit east on one of the small trails through the park to Little Raven Street. Or, continue north to the skateboard park. Take a left and cross the footbridge at 19th Street over the river. While on the bridge, catch views to the north of Denargo Market and the old flour mill. To the south, catch scrumptious upriver views of the Platte and downtown Denver.

At the end of the footbridge, take a left and go down the ramps to the Platte River Trail. Continue to the right, making your way back toward REI, or south along the Platte. You may experience some construction along the way. If necessary, take the steps at the 15th Street pedestrian bridge up to 15th Street. Walk along the 15th Street promenade to Platte Street. Take a left and continue back to the REI parking lot to finish your walk. Or, if there is no construction, continue along the Platte River until you reach the bridge over the confluence where you began this adventure.

DENVER:
CONFLUENCE PARK CLOVER

19. Denver: First Creek at DEN Open Space Out-n-Back

RATING	Easy
DISTANCE	3.8 miles
TIME	1 hour 45 minutes
ELEVATION GAIN	Minimal
USAGE	Part of the regional trail system, you'll find mostly walkers on this trail.

COMMENTS: Despite its awkward name, this short, hidden gem on the way to Denver International Airport offers up many wildlife surprises. Denver Park and Rec manages the trail, but Denver International Airport (thus the DEN in the trail's name) owns the land. Abutted to the Rocky Mountain Arsenal Wildlife Refuge, this 2-mile concrete trail parallels First Creek and abruptly ends as it awaits its extension to the High Line Canal Trail in Green Valley Ranch. This is a great walk during sunset.

The trail runs north out of the trailhead parking lot for about 0.3 mile along the wildlife refuge. Eventually, bison may be seen as the herd expands its range. In the meantime, plenty of hawks, eagles in the winter, and migratory birds skim the horizon. Prairie dogs bark non-stop from the very large colony on the east side of Buckley Road before you reach the right turn to the trail at First Creek. Within the next few years, you'll be able to access the wildlife refuge from its east side rather than driving to the visitor center.

GETTING THERE: The trailhead parking lot is at the corner of Peña Boulevard and 56th Avenue in Denver. Take I-70 to the Peña Boulevard exit 285, go north 2.3 miles and exit on to

The First Creek at DEN trail is a hidden gem.

Peña Boulevard. Turn west (left) and the trailhead is just on the north (right) side of the street. There are no facilities at the trailhead. The parking lot the corner of Peña Blvd. and 56th Ave is pebble and dirt. Look for the sign that says, "First Creek at DEN Open Space."

THE ROUTE: Once parked, admire the prairie dog colony to the north of the parking lot and the interpretation sign just to the west of the parking lot. Take the abandoned Buckley Road street bed north about 0.3 mile. You'll reach an 8-foot-wide concrete path on the right, which is where the First Creek at DEN Open Space trail begins.

   Once along the creek, the trail meanders for just about 2 miles under Peña Boulevard, the A-Train trestle, 56th Avenue, and Tower Road. Despite these major underpassings, the creek bed offers a nice respite of cottonwoods, bee balm, and short grasses. There's even a throwback to the rural area via a horse corral and stable. Keep your eyes peeled for burrowing owls, bald eagles, and other larger birds as you walk along short to medium grasses.

A nice evening stroll can catch gorgeous sunsets over the Rockies.

The trail parallels the creek until you cross it on a low-lying bridge where the creek widens out. Continue along the trail until you pass through a double-arched bridge under Tower Road. On your right will be a nice water feature of flat rocks that invites you to take off your shoes and take a break. It's also the trail's temporary end until it is extended to the High Line Canal Trail. When you're ready, walk back to the trailhead while admiring the vast views of the Rockies the entire way.

Denver International Airport's boundary is the largest geography of any US Airport, and within it, there are enough solar panels to offset about 6% of the total energy consumption at the airport. For a short time between when the old Denver Airport, known as Stapleton, was due to close and the opening of the new airport, travelers used the official airport code of DVX to denote the new Denver airport. Once the old Stapleton airport had its last departure, the new Denver International adopted DEN as its airport code, left over from the old Stapleton location.

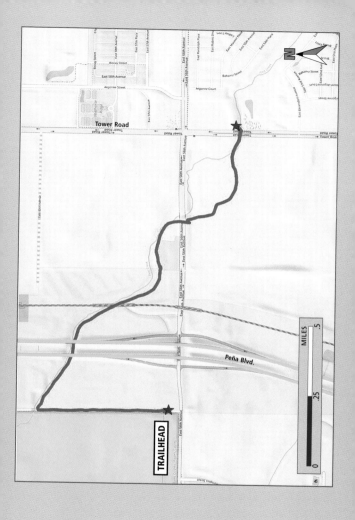

DENVER:
FIRST CREEK AT DEN OPEN SPACE OUT-N-BACK

95

20. Denver: Lowry Park Loop

RATING	Easy
DISTANCE	2.4 miles
TIME	1 hour
ELEVATION GAIN	Minimal
USAGE	Part of the neighborhood sidewalk system and Lowry reservoir, you'll find walkers and joggers along this route.

COMMENTS: For bird lovers, this short nature loop where the old Lowry Field used to be offers up fantastic opportunities to see large and small migrating birds. In the floodplain of the Aurora-Kelley Road Reservoir, tall marsh grasses invite many species of birds for your delightful review. The trail loops up the dam and provides great 360-degree views of Denver.

GETTING THERE: From I-70, take Quebec Street south to E. 6th Avenue Parkway. Turn left (east), then turn right on Uinta Way. Turn left on E. Lowry Boulevard and left again into Great Lawn Park. Park at 101 Yosemite St., Denver near the restrooms.

THE ROUTE: This routes shapes roughly into a figure 8. You'll walk up the left side of the 8 and then down the right.

From the restrooms, take the sidewalk to the left around the small pond. The path will veer north on the west side of the pond. Stay on the sidewalk, passing behind Bishop Machebeuf High School. Pass by a giant sundial on your right, and continue north on the crusher-fine trail along the creek for a 100 feet then veer to your left. You'll be walking along the floodplain of the reservoir. As you approach the dam, you can either take the steps up the dam, veer to the left to go behind the dam,

The old Lowry field provides a nice stroll.

or veer to the right to go in front of the dam. Depending on the trail conditions in the winter, you may only be able to go up the stairs to the top of the dam.

Go up the stairs and cross the top of the dam. Enjoy the views all around, including fantastic views to the west of downtown Denver and the Rocky Mountains. Continue to the east side of the dam, where you can either take the stairs down to the floodplain or cross over the spillway.

Cross the spillway and turn right to walk down the east side of the floodplain, which is also the right side of the figure 8. Follow the trail back to the sundial, veering to the left of the sundial. Continue back to Great Lawn Park, veering to your right and ultimately walking on the sidewalk back to the restrooms.

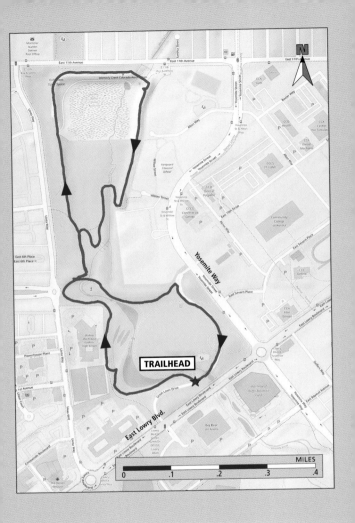

TRAILHEAD

DENVER:
LOWRY PARK LOOP

21. Denver: Rocky Mountain Arsenal Wildlife Refuge

RATING	Moderate
DISTANCE	4 miles
TIME	2.5 hours
ELEVATION GAIN	Minimal
USAGE	The soft surface trails within the Refuge only allow walking, and not dogs are allowed.

COMMENTS: From an army base that made weapons to the largest Superfund site in the country, the Rocky Mountain Arsenal Wildlife Refuge shines in the success of rebirth. Now almost 23 square miles, the refuge invites visitors to view bison, deer, hawks, eagles, prairie dogs, and ferrets. Folks can catch and release fish in its two well-stocked ponds, and hikers can enjoy over 15 miles of trails. Views of Denver can be seen from the southwestern corner of the refuge, and the Rocky Mountains crown the western views. Plains and prairies round out the eastern views. With the abundance of wildlife in the refuge, this is a must-enjoy area of Denver.

GETTING THERE: Take I-70 to Quebec Street and go north to Prairie Parkway. Go right to Gateway Boulevard and turn left and follow the signs to the visitor center, 6550 Gateway Rd., Commerce City. Although the visitor center has limited hours, the refuge is open every day from sunrise to sunset.

THE ROUTE: Once you've parked, enjoy the visitor center and its display of rich history regarding POWs, mustard gas, and habitat restoration. When you're ready, check the binoculars

The lakes at Rocky Mountain Arsenal Wildlife Refuge.

at the large northern-facing window. You may catch a bison at the cistern just beyond the visitor center. Exit the rear of the visitor center and locate the trailhead to the left of the ferret display. Stop by and say hello to the ferrets, then begin your hike along the soft-surfaced Legacy Trail to the east. The trail will head a bit to the north to get close to the cistern and then continues to the east.

Watch for bison to the north. Although the trail does not go into the roaming area of the bison, the herd often hangs out to the north of the fence that runs along the trail. The trail will rise slightly then drop down into a stand of trees. Within

The lakes at Rocky Mountain Arsenal Wildlife Refuge.

the stand, look for mule deer and white-tailed deer. Continue along the trail as it dips down and crosses Wildlife Drive. Bald Eagle nests are off to the east, so be sure to watch for those and red-tailed hawks as well.

Cross the road, veer right and then left to the gazebo. You'll be on the north side of Lake Mary, a small, well-stocked fishing lake. Continue to the left and cross the floating bridge and then turn left to go up the stairs to Lake Ladora. If you would like to add length to this walk, take the Lake Ladora loop for 1.8 miles. Otherwise, turn left and walk along the edge of the lake to the next set of stairs at the parking lot. You'll also find

Be sure to take the trail across Lake Mary.

a composting toilet in the parking lot. Turn left at the head of the parking lot and either take the stairs down to Lake Mary or the access road to the right.

At the bottom of the stairs, continue back toward the gazebo or go around Lake Mary to the left. Either way, you'll come back to Wildlife Road. Cross it again, and follow the path back the way you came. Continue to look for deer in the trees and bison to the north while admiring the expansive views of both downtown Denver and the Rocky Mountains. At the cistern, remember to veer to the left back to the visitor center.

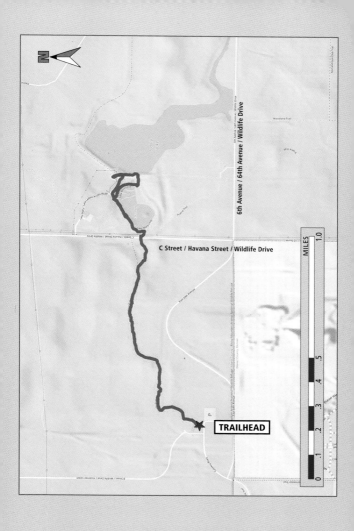

6th Avenue / 64th Avenue / Wildlife Drive

C Street / Havana Street / Wildlife Drive

TRAILHEAD

MILES

0   .1   .2   .3   .4   .5   1.0

22. Denver: South Cherry Creek

RATING	Easy
DISTANCE	2.75 miles
TIME	1 hour
ELEVATION GAIN	Minimal
USAGE	Part of the regional trail system, you'll find walkers, bikers and joggers along this route. Parts of the walk are on neighborhood sidewalks without bikes.

COMMENTS: The Cherry Creek Trail, named after the choke cherry bushes that frequent its banks, buzzes with cycling commuters all day long, making it a bit difficult for pedestrians to walk on its concrete. Most pedestrians stay off the trail and use the unofficial dirt social trails on both sides. But just south of where Cherry Creek intersects with the High Line Canal is a short loop trail that takes walkers through Hampden Heights and avoids the craziness of the Cherry Creek Trail.

GETTING THERE: Take I-225 to Parker Road then go north to E. Dartmouth Avenue and take a left. Take another left on S. Kenton Street and take it to the end and park at the end of the street at the trailhead to the Cherry Creek Trail. There is no need to go into the ball field complex.

THE ROUTE: Once you've parked, notice the Cherry Creek Trail to your west. You can take it to the left and up the dry side of the Cherry Creek Reservoir, or take it the much prettier way to the right. Immediately the trail slopes downhill, passing the John F. Kennedy Golf Course on your left and apartment buildings on the right. The trail will veer to the left as it makes its

There's always a good view on any trail in Denver.

way under Havana and then pops up north of Havana just in time to cross a long pedestrian bridge over the golf course.

Continue along Cherry Creek, enjoying the shade of cottonwoods about 0.25 mile until you come to a sign that points to Hampden Heights to the left. Take the left and catch a straight-as-an-arrow asphalt trail through Hampden Heights. This wonderful linear park through the neighborhood invites you to several benches and places to catch a respite. Neighbors walking dogs say hello and greet you warmly.

At the T in the trail, you'll be at Hampden Heights Park. Turn right and continue to the Cherry Creek Trail, crossing a well-marked neighborhood street. Upon reaching Cherry Creek, turn right. This area of the trail can be busy with cyclists, so take advantage of the dirt social trail along both sides. You'll be walking through Hentzell Park, a park that locals have fought long and hard to keep as a park. Continue for 0.5 mile and you'll be back at the intersection where you split off to go through Hampden Heights.

Retrace your steps back along Cherry Creek Trail, abutting the John F. Kennedy Golf Course until reaching your starting point. If you have additional time, crossover the reservoir and enjoy the inviting Cherry Creek State Park and its bevy of trails as well.

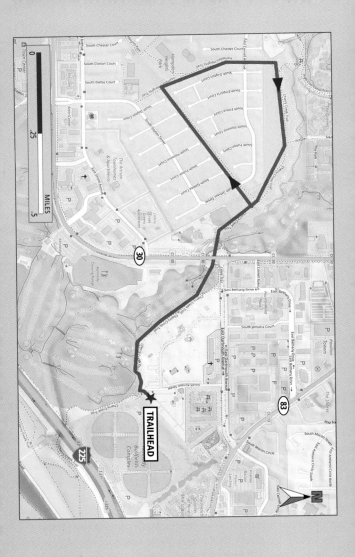

TRAILHEAD

23. Denver: Stapleton Central Park

RATING	Easy
DISTANCE	3 miles
TIME	1 hour
ELEVATION GAIN	Minimal
USAGE	Part of the regional trail system, you'll find walkers, bikers and joggers along this route. Expect families, small children on bikes, and many dog walkers.

COMMENTS: Central Park, one of Denver's largest urban parks, offers miles of trails through the historic Stapleton Airport grounds. Scraped in the '90s and then re-urbanized into a walkable community, Stapleton Airport stood for decades as Denver's gateway to the West. The flight tower still harks as a landmark and is now a restaurant. All around the tower and into Central Park, the Stapleton neighborhood invites all ages to walk and bike its miles and miles of trails, including escapes along Sand Creek and Westerly Creek. This particular route takes you past the Stapleton flight tower and gives views into where the old runways used to be.

GETTING THERE: Central Park Rec Center is a great place to start any walk within Central Park. Take I-70 to Central Park Boulevard. Go south to MLK Jr. Boulevard and turn left. The rec center, at 9651 M.L.K. Jr. Blvd., Denver, will be about 1.0 mile ahead on the left.

THE ROUTE: You can access the trail from the left side of the rec center. Walk along the concrete trail, veering to the right, passing the backside of the rec center. Cross the most eastern

Great walks await you in Stapleton.

Evening is a great time to get in an urban hike.

pedestrian bridge over Westerly Creek, then go up a slight hill. At the fork, go left and walk parallel to the creek to the west.

Before crossing MLK Jr. Boulevard, go right. You'll be paralleling the boulevard. At the first right, cut back into the park, going diagonally until you reach the next major path intersection and go to the left. Follow this path along for about 0.5 mile. You'll walk past soccer fields, a kid's playground, and a rock-climbing wall. Take a slight detour by turning left and enjoy the Alzheimer's Remembrance Garden. Return back from your detour and continue to the left until you reach Central Park Boulevard. Enjoy a close-up view of the old Stapleton Airport's flight tower.

Turn right on Central Park Blvd. Go to the next major path intersection and turn right. Continue enjoying the native grasses, then take a sharp left and go around the sledding hill. Take a right and continue past the backside of the sledding hill, with the park on your right and homes on your left. Continue until you see the trail jut out into a dead-end bridge that overlooks the entire park. You'll see where the runways used to be that taxied the planes north across the Interstate. Enjoy the view, then come back and go to your right to go under the jutting bridge. Go left and continue along the perimeter of the park until you come to the next major trail intersection. There's a nice circle of stones to enjoy a break, or take a right there and head back west to the rec center. Cross the pedestrian bridge you originally crossed, head up the hill, and go around the west side of the rec center to return to your starting point.

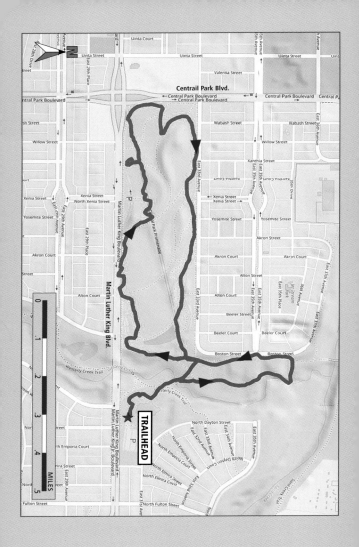

DENVER:
STAPLETON CENTRAL PARK

24. Golden: Lichen Peak North Table Mountain

RATING	Difficult
DISTANCE	4.1 miles
TIME	1 hour 30 minutes
ELEVATION GAIN	581 feet
USAGE	Mostly soft surface trails, you'll find walkers and rock climbers along this route with an occasional biker.

COMMENT: Folks from Golden will argue over which mesa is better to hike—North Table Mountain or South Table Mountain. Both have about the same elevation gain, both take you to the top of a flat mesa, and both give you good views of Golden and Denver. But North Table Mountain gets the vote for the better of the two due to its variety of hiking options on the top of the mesa, its better facilities at the trailhead, and its unique places like Sea Glass and Lichen Point.

Although the climb to the top of North Mountain is steep and difficult, as is the way down, the middle of this walk is easy. With wide-open views and flat trails, wandering on top of the mesa could go on for miles and hours. This particular route has a variety of surface trails from simple dirt to crusher-fine to gravel, so wear your more protected shoes with a rigid sole to manage the rocky surfaces. At the highlight to this trail, you'll climb to Lichen Peak and be rewarded with some of the best 360-degree views of the Front Range. This trail is best done in calm, dry weather, as there are few places to shelter in case of high winds or lightning.

Looking northwest from North Table Mountain.

GETTING THERE: Take I-70 to State Highway 58 toward Golden. Exit right on CO-93. Right before Hog Back Road on the left, you'll see a sign for the North Table Mountain trailhead on the right at 4758 Highway 93, Golden. Take a right into the parking lot where there are restrooms and maps.

THE ROUTE: When you're ready, head straight up the mountain on the service road for about a 0.5 mile. At the top of the road, you can go to the right and see the Sea Cliffs where the climbers go, or veer to the left along Tilting Mesa Trail. Go to the left and then in about 500 feet and you'll see the trailhead for Lichen Peak.

Take the left and head up to Lichen Peak. Stay on the trail and enjoy some of the interpretive signs about lichen and its symbiotic relationship with algae. Continue 0.2 mile to the rocky crag and climb to its peak. You'll see many types of lichen and algae on the rocks as you get to the height of the mesa. Look to your east for scrumptious views of Denver, to the north up the Boulder valley, to the south toward Golden, and to the west at Hogback Ridge. Once you've gotten your fill of the views, head back down the Lichen Peak trail to its head and turn left on Tilting Mesa Trail.

Coming off North Table Mountain looking to the north.

Continue walking along Tilting Mesa Trail, with Denver in your view the entire way as you head northeasterly. After another 0.5 mile, you'll come suddenly upon a small duck pond on your left. Remember to look to your west to catch picturesque views of the duck pond up against the foothills. Continue along until you come to a fork in the trail at Mesa Top Trail. At this point, you can go to the left, cutting off about 0.5 mile of this walk, or go to the right.

Go to the right down Mesa Top Trail, getting closer to the edge of the mesa. You'll come to another fork in the trail. If you go right, you'll head down a one-way trip to the edge of the mesa, bringing you back to the fork. Or, if you've already had enough of the Denver views, take a left. The trail will head northwesterly and then turn to the west, catching back up with the Titling Mesa Trail. Stay to the right when you reach Tilting Mesa.

As steep as it was to come up from the trailhead, you'll now be going down almost as steeply. Continue down the north side of Table Mountain, enjoying views of the Boulder valley and Hogback Ridge. When you've almost reached the bottom of the mountain, you'll catch the North Table Loop trail to the left. This trail meanders along the edge of the mountain, crossing a pedestrian bridge, and making a slow, gradual descent back to the parking lot.

Lichen, which you'll see along the Lichen Peak portion of this hike, form a symbiotic relationship between fungus and single-celled algae. Slow growing at less than 1 mm per year, they are a very fragile species that you can easily trample with the slightest footprint. Lichens grow at all elevations and many types of surfaces, so keep your eye out for other colors and textures elsewhere on top of Table Mountain.

If you have extra time, stop by the American Mountaineering Center at 710 10th Street to visit the headquarters of the Colorado Mountain Club, tour the American Mountaineering Museum ($5 for adults, $1 for children under 12), and explore the 20,000 books in the American Alpine Club Library.

25. Golden: Tucker Gulch Hogback Ridge

RATING	Moderate
DISTANCE	3.45 miles
TIME	1 hour 30 minutes
ELEVATION GAIN	546 feet
USAGE	Part of the neighborhood sidewalk system, you'll find walkers and joggers along this route.

COMMENTS: This fun hike up the ridge goes along a creek, past the historic Brickyard House, through a new Golden neighborhood, and by a tiny craft brewery specializing in gluten-free beers. Along the way there are fantastic views of Hogback Ridge and Golden. With porta-potties at the beginning and end of the walk and some shade throughout, this walk is good any time of the year. A special thanks to Saoirse Charis-Graves and Rhiannon Gallagher at Walk2Connect for sharing this hike.

GETTING THERE: Take I-70 west to County Road 58. Exit to the right on Washington Street and then take a right on Iowa Street. Take a left on North Ford Street and park at Norman D Park on the left at 602 N. Ford St., Golden.

THE ROUTE: Park at Norman D Park, then find the Tucker Gulch Trail at the east end of the park next to the portable toilet. Head west, uphill. You'll walk through the park past a playground. Continue up the hill past the homes and under County Road 93. Follow the trail up the hill, then cross the Golden Gate Canyon Road. Continue on the sidewalk along Catamount Drive. On your right you'll see the historic Brickyard House. Built as a way to showcase the

A gem of a trail in Golden.

different types of bricks one could buy to build a home, this Foursquare Romanesque building dates to the 1890s.

Continue up the hill along the sidewalk. Cross Pine Ridge Road and take an immediate right. In about 100 feet, you'll see a pebble trail to the left. Head up the pebble trail. On your right will be an historic entrance to a retired mine, which is now closed. Walk up the hill another 0.3 mile, take a left on Pine Ridge Road and then veer to the left on Jesse Lane through the neighborhood. Continue along the sidewalk, veer left on Lou's Loop, left on Jesse Lane, then right on Catamount. You'll be back at the intersection of Catamount and Pine Ridge Road. Here you can either continue down Pine Ridge and return to the end of your walk, or take a detour to a small craft brewery.

If you decide to go to the brewery, take a left on Pine Ridge Road. Go one block, take a left on Brickyard Road, walk another block, take a right on Brickyard Circle. At the bottom of the street on the right is a small brewery called Holidaily (801 Brickyard Circle, Golden), which is completely gluten-free. Grab yourself a pint, then head back up the way you came by backtracking along Brickyard Road to Catamount. At Catamount, turn left on Pine Ridge Road and continue back to the parking lot of Norman D Park.

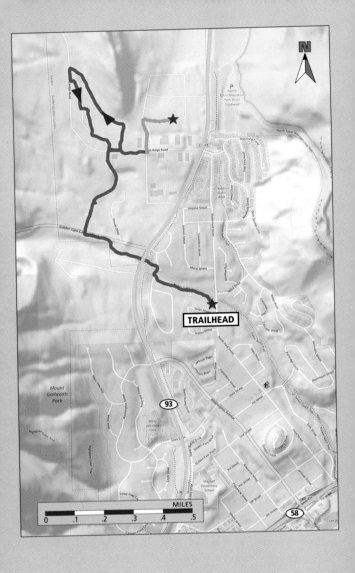

TRAILHEAD

GOLDEN:
TUCKER GULCH HOGBACK RIDGE

26. Lakewood: Belmar Park Loop

RATING	Easy
DISTANCE	3.5 miles
TIME	1 hour 30 minutes
ELEVATION GAIN	Minimal
USAGE	Part of the regional trail system, you'll find walkers, bikers and joggers along this route.

COMMENTS: With such variety and fun, this trail is great with the family or for an evening stroll. In addition, during the holidays, Belmar puts up lights around the historic buildings at the Heritage Center and along the trails to invite a frolic along the lake. With the large Kountze Lake in the middle of the former Bonfils Estate, it's really hard to go wrong while walking in this park. Whether you want to follow the designated route and stay on the very perimeter of the park or meander through the many twists and turns around the lake, you'll definitely want to make your way to the east side of the lake. There you'll find two wonderful "avenues" to walk within the park where Belmar has moved historic buildings to the Heritage Center. Travel through time from the 1800s through the early 1940s as you experience the art and architecture of period buildings and their well-done interpretation.

This route includes a jut under S. Wadsworth Boulevard to take you on a sidewalk meander to Pierce Street. Although not a very thrilling part of the walk, it's an important segment. Eventually, this sidewalk will connect as a trail to the Weir Gulch Trail beyond Pierce, taking you another 5–6 miles along good trail up to Barnam Water Park. If you are not interested in seeing the future connection, bypass going through the tunnel and continue up to the historic Heritage Center to finish the walk.

Belmar Park has many historic buildings.

GETTING THERE: Take US-6 to S. Wadsworth Boulevard and go south. Turn right on W. Virginia Avenue and take the second left in the traffic circle. Park at Belmar Library at 555 S. Allison Pkwy., Lakewood.

THE ROUTE: Once you've parked, walk behind the back of the library. You'll immediately see the trail. Take it to the right. Soon you'll veer around to the left, passing a natural play area and getting great views of Kountze Lake and the foothills. At one time, Mary Bonfils Stanton kept deer and peacocks on this beautiful land when the lake was larger.

As you reach the west side of the park, veer to the left continuing south. The trail will go down a hill and cross over Weir Gulch. At any point, you can take the smaller trails that head the lake or continue around the perimeter trail. Enjoy the large cottonwoods and willows along the gulch and the open views along the rolling hills at the southern end of the park. Cross over the gulch, and then you can either walk up the hill to the Heritage Center or continue to the east under S. Wadsworth. For this route, tunnel under S. Wadsworth and continue on the sidewalk to S. Pierce Street.

At Pierce, notice the horses across the street. Plans are in the works to connect the sidewalk to the Weir Gulch Trail, only about 1.0 mile east from this intersection. Once it's connected, you'll be able to continue along Weir Gulch Trail to Barnam Water Park.

Turn around and return via the tunnel. Veer to your right as you leave the tunnel and head up the hill to the Heritage Center. The first building you'll see is a large red barn. Walk past it to enter the older historic section of the Heritage Center. Walk through the "avenue" and enjoy the interpretation of the old house, schoolroom, farm, water pump, and garage. Past the garage, take a left up the small brick trail and then turn left at the historic Belmar ticket office.

You'll be walking along the other "avenue"; this one dates to the 1920s–1940s, where you can see an original diner, hotel, and gas station. Be sure to stop and read the interpretation and marvel at how all the buildings and a few neon signs were safely moved and gingerly restored. Once you've finished the historic review, walk past the amphitheatre on your left and up the hill to the lake. See remnants of the old marble boathouse.

After enjoying the birds and lake views, continue up the hill and then right, back to the library where you parked. As a side note, while walking through the Heritage Center, you may want to make note of the special events and concerts coming up, including holiday light events and summer concerts.

Belmar Park preserves some of Denver's historic neon signs.

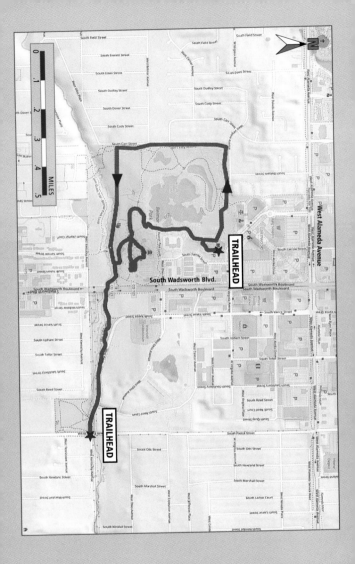

LAKEWOOD:
BELMAR PARK LOOP

27. Lakewood: Mt. Carbon Loop at Bear Creek Lake

RATING	Difficult
DISTANCE	6.6 miles
TIME	2 hours 30 minutes
ELEVATION GAIN	515 feet
USAGE	Part of the park's trail system, you'll find walkers, bikers and joggers along this route.
FEES	$10

COMMENTS: Although the majority of this trail is hot and shadeless, the effort is worth it due to the amazing views from the top of Mt. Carbon. With the foothills of the Rockies to the west and a straight-shot view of downtown Denver to the east, you can get a real feel for the surrounding beauty that Denver offers. In addition, with the west end of Lakewood in clear sight from the top of Mt. Carbon, urban hiking truly takes hold in this wonderful park just minutes from the suburbs. The best time of year to do this hike is in the fall to enjoy the cottonwood colors and cooler temperatures.

GETTING THERE: Take E-470 to Morrison Road and exit east. Entry to Bear Creek Lake Regional Park at 15600 W. Morrison Rd., Lakewood will be immediately on the right. Pay the entrance fee, enter the park, take the first right and then the first right into Skunk Hollow parking lot. The trailhead is on the east end of the parking lot. If you are looking at the information board, turn around. The trailhead is directly behind you.

THE ROUTE: Head east out of the parking lot and immediately cross the road you came in on. You'll come to a T in the trail.

Many urban hikes have rural features.

Look for the Mt. Carbon Loop sign. You can go left or right. Go to the right and continue through the woods. The dirt trail will follow the creek for a very short time and then exit into the full sun. You'll be on the dirt trail in the full sun for almost the entire walk.

The trail continues alongside the park's perimeter road, inching along with the creek on your left and the road on your right. At about 2.0 miles, you'll cross by the park's corrals of rental horses. Continue along, cross W. Hampden Avenue, and you'll come to another set of woods. These trees feed off of Turkey Creek, which will stay to your right as you continue toward Mt. Carbon. You'll take a right, cross Turkey Creek, and then emerge back into the full sun. Here, many mountain bikers pick up the trail to head up Mt. Carbon.

Mt. Carbon will be in front of you. Possibly the highest spot in urban Denver, it's not that ominous being just about 300 feet tall. Prior to your ascent, enjoy Bear Creek Lake. Formed by the reservoir that was built in response to frequent and historical flooding in this area, it's a wonderful place to come back to and fish. Continue upward along the switchbacking trail. At the top, grab a nice view from the benches or picnic table. The foothills will be to your west, and downtown Denver will be to the east.

Denver in view from Mt Carbon.

After taking a break, continue uphill for about 50 feet. Around the bend, you'll see restrooms and fresh water offered up from the co-habitation with Homestead Golf Course. Refill your water bottle, then continue down the west side of Mt. Carbon, which is arguably the nicest part of the trail with Denver views off in the eastern distance. You'll also overlook more of the golf course and top the dam of the reservoir. The trail continues down and below the dam, running parallel to the dam for about 0.5 mile along Kumpfmiller Drive.

Continue along the trail and then back up the north end of the reservoir. Once again you'll top out, and then you'll continue again down the lake side of the reservoir along a single-track bike lane, which is still labeled Mt. Carbon Loop. Watch for coyotes in the knee-high grasses as you continue to descend back toward Bear Creek. You'll cross Kumpfmiller Drive and soon be back in the cottonwoods. Shortly, you'll begin walking along Bear Creek. Keep your eyes open for mule deer and fishermen as you continue along the trail back to the trailhead in the Skunk Hollow parking lot.

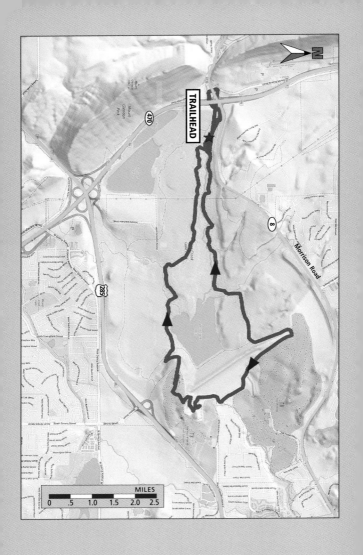

LAKEWOOD:
MT. CARBON LOOP AT BEAR CREEK LAKE

28. Littleton: Lee Gulch to Carson Nature Center

RATING	Easy
DISTANCE	3.8 miles
TIME	1 hour 30 minutes
ELEVATION GAIN	Minimal
USAGE	Part of the regional trail system, you'll find walkers, bikers and joggers along this route. Bikers generally stay on the hard surface, and walkers generally stay on the soft surface of the trails.

COMMENTS: The beauty of the Lee Gulch and the Mary Carter Trails is that you can jump on them almost anywhere and walk as far as you want. Exiting either trail is easy, with access to many bus stops and easy-to-find, pick-up areas. Whereas most of Lee Gulch has good shade and mostly walkers, Mary Carter Greenway is mostly sunny with many cyclists both training and commuting. Together, the two trails form a nice urban amble for any time of the year.

GETTING THERE: Although you can get onto the Lee Gulch Trail from a variety of places, including an intersection with the High Line Canal, a good place to start is Carbone Park. Be careful about parking between 9–3 during weekdays, as it's permit required. But even if you are there during these times, you can find parking in the 7500 block of S. Elati Street, Littleton. Once parked, access the trail up through Carbone Park or where it crosses Elati Street. For this particular hike, park along Elati and join Lee Gulch at the bridge at Elati and the trail. To get to 7500 S Elati, take I25 to E Bellevue Ave.

These urban hikes are always with a neighborhood nearby.

Go west to University and take a left, going south. Go west (right) on E Arapahoe Rd. Take a left on S Broadway, a right on W Ridge Road and a left on S Elati Street.

THE ROUTE: Once reaching the trail off Elati, head west along this crusher-fine trail. Immediately you'll see a 10-foot waterfall of the Lee Gulch Creek. Look for small fish in the waterfall's pool. Quickly after the pool you'll see the South Suburban Lee Gulch mile marker 2.3. Continue down the slightly curved path along the creek. Notice the next South Suburban sign pointing out the many access points nearby, including High Line Canal and Puma Park.

Continue along the trail, passing a disc golf course and Runyon Elementary School through Carbone Park. You'll cross the creek and walk along tennis courts with the creek to your right. At the T in the trail, you'll see a sign to the left to South Windermere Street. Stay on the trail by going to the left. Cross the creek again on another footbridge then take a sharp left. As you continue west, you'll have intimate views of the creek, as you'll be right down near the water.

Just past the Lee Gulch mile marker 3.0, you'll pass some private beehives on the south side of the creek and then you'll enter the east end of Ashbaugh Park. A quaint neighborhood pond will greet you, inviting you to sit on one of the benches under the cottonwood tree. Cross South Windermere Street, continue down an elevated path, and pass Lee Gulch mile marker 3.5. The trail shed opens up and you'll start to get a glimpse of the mountains. At the next T in the trail, take the bridge over the creek, enter into Lower Ridgewood Park, pass the playground and tennis courts, and cross over Prince Street. Pass mile marker 4.0, St. Mary's School of Littleton, the Lee Gulch sluice, and a baseball field. Continue along until you come to a set of double tunnels. The trail goes beneath Santa Fe through some old hand-cut stone tunnels and then a modern tunnel. As you come out from under Santa Fe, you'll approach Lee Gulch Overlook as you arrive onto the Mary Carter Greenway intersection. Enjoy the sculpture of a boy fishing, and veer to the left of the bike traffic circle.

You'll now be on the Mary Carter Greenway heading south, with the Platte River on your left. Walk along the crusher-fine trail, which parallels the bike path to your right. Up ahead on your left, you'll see Reynolds Landing. Refill your water bottle, use the facilities, and take a break on the shaded picnic tables. Watch the locals catch fish from the Platte. Whereas Lee Gulch Trail is narrow and intimate, Mary Carter widens and invites many users.

You'll enter the South Platte Park. Notice the South Suburban signs describing the many lakes along the trail, which resulted from gravel pits. A few breweries dot the landscape to the east. Just after the breweries is a small bridge that both pedestrians and cyclists must use. Although the bikes must yield to pedestrians legally, be sure to look to your rear before crossing the bridge. A bit farther, you'll see a sign saying "Welcome to the Northern Wildlife Area." At this point you can either stay on the pedestrian trail or cross over the bike trail and join the Wildlife Trail. This shady trail gets closer to the Platte and away from the bikers. You'll see more birds and small mammals.

The great Denver flood of 1965 swelled the banks of Plum Creek and the Platte River. Inundating many neighborhoods such as Athmar Park, Baker, Auraria, Globeville, and Valverde, among others, the flood destroyed century-old and brand new homes, bridges, and businesses. The flood gave Denver Water the clout to put in the long-needed flood control mechanism of Chatfield Dam, once strongly opposed by nearby residents. In addition, Auraria neighborhood became home to its current three colleges (University of Colorado Denver, Denver Community College, and Metro State University) and the 9th Street Historic District, which preserves several homes of relocated families. Students of families displaced by the Auraria redevelopment and who can claim genealogical lineage to the original Auraria residents receive "Displaced Aurarians" scholarships to attend any of the three schools.

As you walk along the Platte, pay attention for a cut back to the main trail to get to the Carson Nature Center. Outside of the nature center is some great signage describing the history of the sand pits and identifying the peaks of the mountain range to the west. If open, go inside and learn about Mary Carter, the great 1965 flood, and the Carson Center. Use the facilities. If you'd like, continue down the trail or exit here.

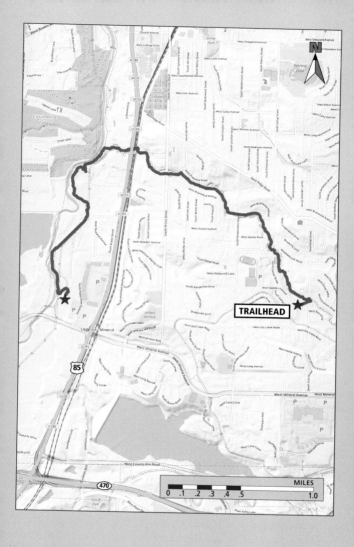

29. Thornton: Four Northern Parks

RATING	Moderate
DISTANCE	5.5 miles
TIME	2 hours 30 minutes
ELEVATION GAIN	350 feet
USAGE	Part of the regional trail system, you'll find walkers, bikers and joggers along this route.

COMMENTS: A very varied hike, this loop takes you through four parks and two cities. Starting in a large prairie dog habitat, you can hear the barking dogs as they alert your passing on the way to a large, multi-functional park with boats, fishing, fields, gardens, and skateboarding where you then wrap around through an open space of rolling hills. At 5.5 miles, you'll pass the time quickly due to the variety of things to see and places to enjoy on your way through four parks.

GETTING THERE: Take I-25 to 104th Avenue exit. Go east about 2.5 miles, crossing Colorado Boulevard. The parking lot will be on the right just past Colorado Boulevard. There are porta-potties in the parking lot.

THE ROUTE: The Grange Hall Trail is just to the west of the parking lot, where the first thing you'll see is a small fishing pond in the Grandview Ponds Open Space. Go to the right and take the path through the tunnel beneath Colorado Boulevard. You'll emerge into the Riverdale Open Space and Prairie Dog Habitat where hundreds of prairie dogs will bark your arrival and nonchalantly get out of your way as you pass by. The trail curves to the right and at the T, take the left.

A curvy adventure awaits ahead.

Continue meandering through the habitat and over the creek. You'll cross E. 108th Avenue and then go under Colorado Boulevard.

Emerging from the tunnel, you'll be in Northglenn and the very large Carpenter Park, named after the previous mayor and council person, Margaret W. Carpenter. This 100+ acre park invites all ages and abilities to enjoy its many recreational options throughout the acreage, including fishing, soccer, kite flying, gardening, and boating. You'll continue on the Grange Hall Trail to the first pedestrian bridge. Take the bridge to the left and then take a right on the trail running along the open grassy field.

Follow along the grassy field to its northern edge and at the large cottonwood, veer to the right and head north. Rather than taking the large pedestrian bridge across Grange Creek, veer to the left and stay along the perimeter trail. The trail follows a rolling hills path with homes on the left and the creek running on the right. Cross over Fox Run Parkway into Stonehocker Park and enjoy the public art, called Desert Mother.

Continue along the perimeter of the trail getting giant views of rolling hills and medium grass prairie. The trail will make a wide sweep to the right, crossing the creek and heading north again toward a tunnel. Before the tunnel, take a right on the white pebble trail down the hill, and then take a right at the T on the soft-surface trail. You'll now be looping back toward Carpenter Park. When you reach Fox Run Parkway again, you'll stay on the sidewalk to the right to cross back over at Desert Mother. Before turning right, though, enjoy the view of the historic Stonehocker Farm and the bison artwork. Cross the street and continue back through Stonehocker Farm.

This time, when you get to the large pedestrian bridge, cross it and take the trail to the left. You'll follow the trail back into Carpenter Park, but veer to the left and go around the lake. At the junction of the next lake, stay to the left and go around that lake as well. If the boats are out, you'll enjoy people boating and fishing. Continue around the lake to the boathouse and find the restrooms and snack bar.

When you've finished at the boathouse, take the trail to the left, keeping the amphitheatre on your left and the lake on your right. Go down the hill back to the open, grassy field and take a left. The Carpenter Center and another playground will be on your left with the grassy field on your right. Go back whence you came through the tunnel under Colorado Boulevard.

Continue back through the prairie dog habitat and through the starting tunnel at 104th Avenue, returning back to your car.

TRAILHEAD

Colorado Blvd

East 10th Avenue

44

MILES

0   .5   1.0   1.5   2.0

30. Westminster: Westminster Loop

RATING	Easy to Moderate
DISTANCE	2.5–6 miles
TIME	1 to 2 hours
ELEVATION GAIN	270 feet
USAGE	Part of the regional trail system, you'll find walkers, bikers and joggers along this route. Parts of this walk also go along the neighborhood sidewalk system which has mostly walkers using it.

COMMENTS: Westminster has developed a wonderful trail system for all ages and abilities. This particular loop takes you up through the open space giving you sneak peaks at a large bird population, coyotes, and prairie dogs. You'll amble along the College Trail, which gives wonderful suggestions for how to enjoy the open space with all of your senses. At the juncture with the Legacy Ridge Trail, you can decide to head back to your car for a 2.5-mile loop, or take Legacy Ridge and take a long, slow, intimate climb up through the neighborhood to reach the Farmers' High Line Canal Trail, which is different than the High Line Canal further south. On this route, you'll then continue down the hill toward the Westminster Recreation Center, making a 6-mile loop.

GETTING THERE: Take US-36 north to Sheridan Boulevard North and turn north (right). Take a left on W. 105th Avenue into the rec center parking area, where the address is 10455 Sheridan Blvd, Westminster, CO. At your first right, you'll see a sign pointing to Big Dry Creek Trailhead to the right. Follow those signs to the end of the road. Park just north of the porta-potties and look for the trailhead just to the east of the lake.

Some urban hikes through neighborhoods can be quiet getaways.

The Flatirons off to the northwest.

THE ROUTE: Locate the trailhead just to the east of the lake and take the pedestrian bridge to the east. Just beyond the disc golf fairway, follow the Big Dry Creek Trail to the right. You'll be on a concrete path with homes on the left and a creek bed on your right. You'll cross the creek and then walk under Sheridan Boulevard. Right after passing under the street, you'll enter a giant thistle garden that in the spring explodes with purple blooms and in the fall offers up wonderful, prickly textures against yellow cottonwood leaves. Pass the Cotton Creek Trail and Legacy Ridge Trail, continuing along Big Dry Creek.

Pass under W. 112th Avenue. A ball park will be on your left as you climb the short rise on a crusher-fine trail with wonderful views out across the creek bed. Watch for coyotes, prairie dogs, and magpies. Front Range Community College sits on the hill to the south. You'll pass the turn for College Trail. Keep going, and the Big Dry Creek Trail will make a large, sweeping turn to the right. At the bottom of the hill, stop and learn about the history of Big Dry Creek and the Calkins Ditch. Cross the creek and turn to the right onto College Trail. Big Dry Creek will continue to the left.

Along College Trail, enjoy the suggestions of how to engage with the trail and its environs. The college posts up seasonal suggestions for habitat to find, scents to smell, and images to enjoy. Continue along College Trail, catching big, wide views of the Flatirons. Cross over the pedestrian bridge and then veer to the left to join back up with the Big Dry Creek Trail. Continue back west toward the way you came. If you so choose, continue back along your original path to your car, walking about 2.5 miles in a loop.

Or, if you'd like to expand the loop to 6 miles, take the left off College Trail onto Big Dry Creek Trail. Continue back under W. 112th, then take the left at Legacy Ridge Trail. Say goodbye to the open space and say hello to the concrete sidewalk that journeys uphill through the Cotton Creek neighborhood to the Legacy Ridge Golf Course. Near the top of the hill, take a right, continuing the short distance up the hill and along the golf course. The trail will end at the golf course driving range. Look to your right for the sign that says "Bike Path" and follow the sidewalk through the parking lot about 100 feet. You'll see a sign for the Farmers' High Line Canal.

On the bridge over the High Line Canal, check for water that might be flowing to service some of the fields downstream. The Farmers' High Line Canal, built in the 1860s, follows the highest topographical line and carries water to thirsty farmland. Now, it invites you to take a right and follow it along the meandering sidewalk next to Legacy Ridge Parkway.

Cross over several residential intersections as you make your way to W. 104th Avenue and take a right, staying along the sidewalk, with the avenue on your left and the golf course on your right. At Sheridan Boulevard, cross over Sheridan and then take a right. Walk along the sidewalk to the rec center, following the sidewalk up into the rec center, out to the lake, and then follow the trail to the right along the lake until you reach your car. Before leaving, be sure to take in the vast views of Long's Peak and the Flatirons.

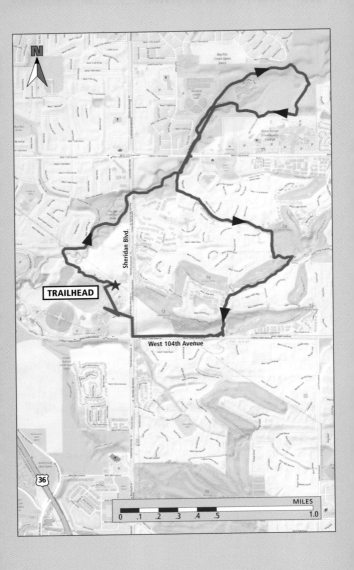

WESTMINSTER:
WESTMINSTER LOOP

About the Author

Chris Englert, the Walking Traveler and Denver's Urban Hiker, believes walking is the platform for life. Volunteered into wanderlusting at age 5, she's traveled all 50 US states and 52 countries. Although she moved to Denver in 2013, she has quickly become an expert on Denver's urban hikes, walking all of its major trails and all 78 Denver neighborhoods, plus the surrounding Aurora, Arvada, Wheat Ridge, Golden, Thornton, and Littleton. Chris shares her love of walking while traveling via blogs, books, and presentations. A natural storyteller, she invites you along as she explores Denver and the world, one walk at a time. You can follow her on social media at @UrbanHikingDen.

Checklist

Denver: 9 Creeks Loop

Illustration by Jesse Crock

Join Today.
Adventure Tomorrow.

The Colorado Mountain Club helps you maximize living in an outdoor playground and connects you with other adventure-loving mountaineers. We summit 14ers, climbs rock face, work to protect the mountain experience and educate generations of Coloradans.